The Prison and the Pinnacle

Papers to commemorate the
Tercentenary of
Paradise Regained and *Samson Agonistes*
Read at
The University of Western Ontario
March-April 1971

PUBLISHED BY UNIVERSITY OF TORONTO PRESS
IN ASSOCIATION WITH
THE UNIVERSITY OF WESTERN ONTARIO

The Prison
and
the Pinnacle

EDITED BY BALACHANDRA RAJAN

© University of Toronto Press 1973
Toronto and Buffalo
Printed in Canada
ISBN 0-8020-1929-3
ISBN Microfiche 0-8020-0267-6
LC 72-90737

CONTENTS

CONTRIBUTORS

Arthur Barker

Professor of Renaissance Literature at the University of
Western Ontario. He is the author of *Milton and the Puritan
Dilemma* (1942) and has edited *Milton: Modern Essays in
Criticism* (1965).

Barbara K. Lewalski

Professor of English at Brown University. She is the author
of *Milton's Brief Epic* (1966) and has in the press *John
Donne's Poetry of Praise*. As well, she has edited *Much Ado
About Nothing* in the Blackfriars Shakespeare (1969) and
has co-edited *Seven Poets of the Seventeenth Century* now
in the press.

Balachandra Rajan

Senior Professor of English at the University of Western Ontario. He is the author of *'Paradise Lost' and the Seventeenth Century Reader* (1947), *The Lofty Rhyme: A Study of Milton's Major Poetry* (1970) and *W.B. Yeats: A Critical Introduction* (1965). Edited *'Paradise Lost': A Tercentenary Tribute* (1969). Professor Rajan has also edited books on *T.S. Eliot* (1947) and on *Modern American Poetry* (1950) and has published two novels, *The Dark Dancer* (1958) and *Too Long in the West* (1961).

Irene Samuel

Professor Emerita of Hunter College and currently Andrew Mellon visiting Professor at the University of Pittsburgh. She is the author of *Plato and Milton* (1947) and *Dante and Milton* (1966), and has in press a translation of Tasso's *Discourses on the Heroic Poem* in collaboration with Mariella Cavalchini.

Northrop Frye

University Professor at the University of Toronto. Among his many books are *Fearful Symmetry* (1947), *The Anatomy of Criticism* (1957), *Fables of Identity* (1963), *The Well-Tempered Critic* (1963), *The Educated Imagination* (1963), *T.S. Eliot* (1963), *A Natural Perspective* (1965), *Fools of Time* (1967), *The Modern Century* (1967), *A Study of English Romanticism* (1968), *The Stubborn Structure* (1970), *The Bush Garden* (1971), and *The Critical Path* (1971). *The Return to Eden* (1965) is a study of Milton's two epics.

FOREWORD

This book brings together five papers read at the University of Western Ontario in 1971 to mark the tercentenary of the publication of *Paradise Regained* and *Samson Agonistes*. Five papers read for a similar celebration in 1967 have already been published under the title: *'Paradise Lost.' A Tercentenary Tribute*. The tercentenary of the 1667 volume was extensively celebrated. That of 1671 was less widely observed and Western may be the only university to have marked both tercentenaries by commemorative volumes. The honouring of Milton's three major works at a single university by eminent scholars both Canadian and American is not simply a tribute to the poems. It is also a confirmation that to continue reading them can be part of our life. The fit and not so few audience of teachers and students who heard these papers provided this confirmation, both by their attentiveness and their continuing interest in the series.

In 1967 the tercentenary of *Paradise Lost* chimed with the centenary of confederation and an all-Canadian cast was chosen for the occasion. In 1971 we have been joined by two scholars from the United States known to all Miltonists and to many others. Barbara Lewalski's presence is indispensable when *Paradise Regained* is the poem being discussed; and Irene Samuel, whose association with this university includes the teaching of a summer course here, has taught us to think again on what it means to be the 'utmost of mere man.' Three of the original five – Northrop Frye, Arthur Barker, and the editor – have persevered into the seventies so that the two volumes are linked not only in their subjects but in the kind of attention that the subjects are given. Again, varying contexts are made to surround the poems and as before the rich meaningfulness of the poems is made evident by the manner in which they reach out to what surrounds them. These illuminations of the text do not always result in the text being seen in the same way but even if we fail to agree on what happened on the pinnacle we can still agree that the centre of attention is man, whether perfected in rational self-reliance or in creative dependence on the divine will.

The text is cited from the Columbia edition. The Yale edition is used for the prose. When the Yale text has not so far been published, the Columbia edition is employed. The standard abbreviations are used for learned periodicals.

Our grateful appreciation is due to the Humanities Research Council of Canada, using funds provided by the Canada Council, and to the J.B. Smallman Memorial Research Fund for generously providing the grants which have made possible the publication of this book.

The Prison and the Pinnacle

CALM REGAINED THROUGH PASSION SPENT

The Conclusions of the Miltonic Effort

ARTHUR E. BARKER

$\mathfrak{D}$espite the 'conclusions' indicated by its title, this first discourse in our tercentenary series of lectures must be regarded only as leading off, or leading on, by way of preparatory introduction. We are commemorating the publication of what tradition – though not without recent determined dissent – has regarded as Milton's final poetic communication, in 1671, some four years after the publication of *Paradise Lost*, duly commemorated here by an earlier series and volume, and some three years before Milton's death, which we may well look forward to commemorating under the same distinguished chairmanship and editorship as before and now. Hence we shall be chiefly concerned in this series to celebrate the conclusions of a great, if agitated and agitating, career, and to contemplate their relevance to us three hundred years later. Despite some dissenting voices in his time and ours, we shall be saying that the hopes Milton expressed in the early sixteen-forties, as he reluctantly responded to the challenges of revolutionary effort in an era no less agitated and agitating than ours, were not entirely frustrated: he wrote well thereafter 'in laudable things.' Despite the 'hideous roar' of his times and the 'whelming tide' that has all but overwhelmed in ours the 'old and elegant' humanities he uniformly admired, he has, we shall say, left 'something so written to aftertimes' that they will 'not willingly let it die.'[1]

Yet, the atmosphere of the times being what it then was and now is, our tones are likely to be, as with nearly all commentary on Milton these days, not only solemn but, naturally, elegiac. We are commemorating the conclusive efforts of one of the most venerated of our 'old Bards,' one superior to 'the famous Druids,' perhaps even in some loftily rhyming sense to be associated with those 'holy Sages' who 'once did sing.' Our endeavour will be to make our way through the tangled woods with their shattered leaves, and beyond the disturbing reverberations of dread voices, towards 'the great vision of the guarded Mount' of his last poems. There we shall hope to break out, if not into the sudden blaze of some transcendentally compensating vision, at least into the sustaining serenity of some more or less conclusive 'calm of mind' in which, with 'all passion spent,' we may make our way, tomorrow (and tomorrow and tomorrow) towards 'fresh Woods, and Pastures new.'[2]

This introductory discourse must attempt to prepare the way for that, as that will be illuminated by the distinguished Miltonists it is its privilege to precede – as Renaissance literature preceded Milton and, as some think, reached its monumental conclusion in his poetic career,

1 An Apology, Yale, I, 890; Lycidas, 1.61, I, 78, and 1.157, I, 82; Areopagitica, II, 489; The Reason of Church-government, I, 810
2 Lycidas, 1.53, I, 78; On the Morning of Christ's Nativity, 1.5, I, 1; Lycidas, 1.161, I, 82; Samson Agonistes, 1.1758, I, 399; Lycidas, 1.193, I, 83

though others think that what his career tragically reflects is the frustrated withdrawal of Renaissance idealism into the compensating security of a highly spiritualized inner calm, a Paradise within, as Renaissance expectations resoundingly collapsed into the Philistine shambles of the modern world. And this discourse must prepare the way chiefly by superficially reviewing our two poems, by suggesting what is likely to be our initial response to them in the light of current evaluations of them, and by attempting thereby to indicate some of the preliminary problems to be dealt with in the process of our elegiac memorialization and its transformation, by the lectures to follow, into sustaining celebration. In this introductory endeavour, this discourse is only too likely to seem incapable of rising above the wandering woods and craggy foothills below the Miltonic mount. But in that it may at least prove to be not entirely inconsistent with the preliminaries of the typically Miltonic process, and with the initial demands that process makes on Milton's readers, from the most notable of the early poems, and certainly with *Lycidas*, through the later poems, and not least *Samson Agonistes*. Having now made some effort to sweep the commemorative and associative strings, we should find it profitable to begin our introductory considerations by reflecting on that typically Miltonic process and the demands it makes for the rewards it offers.

The fullest statement we get from Milton about poetry is the apologetic statement in one of his early revolutionary pamphlets, in the preface to the second book of *The Reason of Church Government* of 1642, in which he is claiming his right, through his devoted though incomplete preparations for the composition of major poems, to contribute to the effort to purify the church and so society by uttering, though through the subordinate mode of left-handed prose, a prophetically jarring blast against corruption which will sustain a renewed faith in better

principles and so the effort of reform.[3] Central to his
apologetic statement about the functions of poetry is his
assertion of its power 'to allay the perturbations of the
mind, and set the affections in right tune.' This central
notion about the function of poetry, with its Classical,
Biblical, Renaissance background, is less irrelevant to the
motives of Milton's revolutionary prose and so to his justification of his left-handed efforts than may at first appear
and has sometimes been suggested. The dynamically
informing purpose of the prose throughout is to allay the
perturbations induced by a desperate sense of irreversible
pollution in human affairs and to contribute to the setting
of human affections in the right tune at once essential to
and the reward of sustained reform. In the two-handed, if
not ambidextrous, activities of Milton's literary career, the
controversial prose operations of his left hand are by no
means irrelevant to, and perhaps rather parallel to, and
in some sense certainly preparatory to, the operations of his
poetic right. This is a matter we shall no doubt be led to
reflect upon more fully as our series proceeds, especially
because the Miltonic preface to the second of our poems
begins with a statement about the purgative and tempering
function of tragedy which repeats, in less tentative and
more precise and modifying terms, the notion of poetry's
function expressed in the revolutionary context of some
thirty years earlier. We shall want to consider, in our
interpretation and appraisal of the tragic effect of *Samson
Agonistes*, the full implications of this prefatory statement.[4] And since we are commemorating the publication
of a two-poem volume, we may be led to inquire to what
extent the tragically purgative and tempering principle
may be operative in *Paradise Regained* – or at least the
allaying and tuning principle of the statement of 1642, if

3 *Works*, I, 803–23, and especially 812–17 for the phrase quoted in
  this paragraph and the next
4 *Col.*, I, 331–3

indeed its notions about poetry are applicable to Milton's later poems, in view of the frustratingly and perturbingly tragic pattern of his revolutionary experience.

Most commentators on Milton's poetic achievement make use of the statement of 1642 as an expression of his characteristic guiding principles. Though it is controversially apologetic, tentative at some points, and chiefly concerned with incomplete preparations (which nevertheless, by their very incompleteness as well as their devotedness, qualify him for reforming controversy), its formulation of principles is clearly derived from the achievements of the early poems, especially in what it says of the functions of poetry and of the disciplines and inspiring supports required in the process of composition. It also indicates Milton's main models, both Classical and Biblical. In doing so, and in justifyingly outlining Milton's plans and hopes, it comments on, among other forms, brief epic and 'high and stately Tragedy' in terms that have been stimulating to most commentaries on our poems. Yet all commentators on Milton's post-revolutionary poems have to take into account the differences worked by hard experience in the Miltonic mood between the early sixteen-forties and the sixteen-sixties and sixteen-seventies. Our response to that Miltonic experience of perturbing frustration (and our response to its parallels with our own experience) induces us to believe that the large and largely Christian-humanist statement of poetic principles and purposes surrounding Milton's notion of the allaying and tuning function of poetry in 1642 is to be associated chiefly and perhaps only with his enthusiastically revolutionary Christian-Utopian expectations then, and that the frustration of these expectations by experience and history worked a radically spiritualizing transformation in his Christian-humanist notions about the nature and function of poetry, not least about what it can do for the perturbations of the mind and about the key in which it may set the affections. We are likely to find ourselves inclined to believe that experience taught Milton and teaches us that much of the humanistic purpose reflected in the statement of 1642 must be given up or at any rate radically spiritualized, and that this is the principal burden of the later poems. Among other things, that statement humanistically observes that poetry is 'of power beside the office of a pulpit, to inbreed and cherish in a great people the seeds of vertu, and publick civility....' We are likely to be inclined to think that this, and similarly humanistic notions about the humanizing and civilizing function of poetry, had to be sacrificed by Milton, or at least radically spiritualized, because of the archetypal three-act tragic pattern of his career: first the still-Renaissance, expansively Elizabethan, and sensitively Jacobean period of the early poems; then the twenty years of passionately idealistic and progressively frustrated and embittered revolutionary-prose effort; and last, after the disastrous collapse of high reforming expectations, the isolated despair, in blindness and defeat under the Restoration monarchy, in which the poet withdrawingly folds himself in his protective and compensating singing-robes and out of which the later poems make their more spiritualized and solitary way. We are also likely to be inclined to think that Milton was enforced to spiritualize yet further some of *The Reason of Church Government*'s other, supposedly less humanistic because more Christian, notions of what poetry can do: celebrating 'in glorious and lofty Hymns the throne and equipage of Gods Almightinesse, and what he works, and what he suffers to be wrought with high providence in his [later, of course, entirely spiritualized and other-worldly] Church'; singing also of 'the victorious agonies of Martyrs and Saints,' such as our Samson perhaps, but perhaps no longer, amidst historical failure, presuming to sing of 'the deeds and triumphs of just and pious Nations doing valiantly through faith against

the enemies of Christ' but rather deploring 'the general
[and later, indeed, total] relapses of Kingdoms and States
from justice and Gods true worship.' 'Lastly,' as instrumental to the process of allaying and tuning, though in the
last poems in some more spiritualized and less relevantly
militant way, poetry is said to concern itself with 'whatsoever in religion is holy and sublime, in vertu amiable, or
grave,' though in the last poems with rather less of the
amiable and rather more of severe gravity, and 'whatsoever
hath passion or admiration in all the changes of that which
is call'd fortune from without, or the wily suttleties and
refluxes of mans thoughts from within,' though in the last
poems with a much heavier sense of unfortunate (or paradoxically fortunate) fatality and, we are much inclined
to think, much less concern with subtleties and refluxes
than with the compensations and securities to be found in
withdrawal to the Paradise within. And we may also be
much inclined to think, as a consequence of Milton's perturbing experience and our own academic experience as
humanists, that this spiritualizing transfiguration of poetic
purposes through tragic experience involves some repudiation in the later poems of *The Reason of Church Government*'s humanistic notion that to the inspiration required
for such poetry the poet must responsively add 'industrious
and select reading, steddy observation, insight into all
seemly and generous arts and affaires.' The subtleties and
refluxes of our own critical scholarship, not least as it
concerns our two poems, may incline us to doubt the value
and efficacy of that 'labour and intent study' through which
the idealistically Christian-humanist early Milton supposed the inspired could make their inspiration operative
by 'Teaching over the whole book of sanctity and vertu
through all the instances of example.' In our consideration
of Milton's last poems we are likely to find that what is at
issue, for us as for him, is the relevance of that humane
knowledge which the Renaissance regarded as instrumental

to wisdom, through which it supposed the humanist poet must support and humanize his faith and qualify himself for the performance of his function by becoming himself – as Milton said in another early revolutionary pamphlet – 'a true Poem, that is, a composition, and patterne of the best and honourablest things; not presuming to sing high praises of heroick men, or famous Cities, unlesse he have in himselfe the experience and the practice of all that which is praise-worthy.'[5]

Thus we may formulate, in terms of the differences in emphasis or the continuing relations between Milton's early revolutionary-humanist conceptions of the nature and function of poetry and his later post-revolutionary conceptions as we can discern them in the preface to *Samson Agonistes* and in his performance, some of the questions that are likely to perturb us in our developing appraisal in this commemorative series on the concluding poetic expressions of his effort. These are among the principal questions with which commentary has been and continues to be concerned. What is the place of the Renaissance humanistic ideal and its learning in our two poems? Is it there only to be repudiated, as frustratedly futile, in favour of some more highly spiritualized and poetic vision, or does it still have, at least in some degree, a more positive and still humanizing function? What are these later poems doing with the Classical and Christian elements in Christian-humanist learning, and what can we make for our interpretive purposes of the relation of our poems to the forms and conventions of such Classical and Biblical literary models as the earlier statement admiringly instances, assuming their related place in the Christian-humanist poetic tradition? Are the Classical modes echoed only to throw into relief, and chiefly by contrast, an otherworldly Biblical spirituality? Or does Milton's manipulation of conventional models of both sorts imply some

5 *An Apology*, Yale, I, 890

continuing relation between them in and for humanity?
Have the Christian-humanist ethical principles that so
dynamically inform the earlier statement, with the confident assumption that these are sustained and deepened by
experience, learning, and poetry, gone with the painful
frustration of their revolutionary social applications? Have
they been transfigured by the purgations of harsh experience into the withdrawn because defeated spirituality of
transcendentalized poetic vision? Or does the vision imply
in itself some ethically tempered return to the perturbing
tensions of the common human situation even after cruci-
fied defeat? Or, lastly, to return to the centrally functional
Miltonic concern we began with, which is likely to recur
as a continual undertone in the series of our considerations,
in what terms may these poems relevantly perform for us
the office of allaying the perturbations of the mind in the
face of harsh experience and of setting the affections in
right tune, in the phrases of the earlier statement, or, in the
phrases of the later statement (which is at least biblio-
graphically central to our 1671 volume), the office of purging the mind of 'pity and fear, or terror,' and tempering and
reducing them 'to just measure with a kind of delight...'?
Is there after all, and despite revolutionary defeat, so very
much difference between the implications of the earlier
phrasing and the implications of the later? Is not Milton's
theory of the function of poetry, thus phrased, a function
of his response to experience? And how may we best gain
our poetic reward through our response to his representation of experience and his poetic communication of his
conclusions? To put it in the phrases of the final line of
our 1671 volume (which so many students of Milton have,
rightly or wrongly, wished to regard as his conclusive
statement), what does it mean to have reached a state of
'all passion spent'? Spent in what sense? Drained away?
Exhausted? Spent how? On whose behalf? And for what?
And what exactly is the character of that 'calm of mind'

which we may be led to attempt to achieve for ourselves through our response to these poems, and perhaps thereby – if it is not totally out of order to echo a much earlier poem – through our response even to time and the will of heaven?

This introductory lecture can do little more than formulate such questions and attempt to illustrate them by reviewing their emergence from our poems in the light of critical commentary. It can hardly presume even to suggest answers to them. It must concern itself with the initial stage in the Miltonic poetic process and our response to it, with what perturbs – and is perhaps intentionally designed to perturb – us in our initial response. Clearly, our two poems are, at least initially, thus much concerned – with the efforts of the Satanic tempter to work perturbation in a mind which, wonderfully and in some sense divinely, proves already essentially unperturbable under trial and whose calm is deepened and energized thereby as it proceeds in its contemplation of actions to be undertaken and experiences to be accepted, and with the dreadful perturbations of the Miltonically defeated and enslaved Samson (and his fellows), leading, through purgation and mysteriously rousing motions, to a tempering which revivingly enables him to do valiantly through faith, even unto self-destruction. In this perturbed endeavour, this discourse cannot presume to associate itself even with the prologue of that Attendant Spirit whose confidently superior Platonic idealism provides such an impressive opening for Milton's early masque, however limitedly effective his subsequent explanatory and protective endeavours prove, until he calls up a figure once much more perturbed and now much more restoratively effective than himself. Even less can it associate itself with the discourse of that affable, and indeed amiable, if sometimes grave, archangel, Raphael, whose somewhat Platonized and uncertain account of past history should prepare Adam (and Eve) for the trial to

come, but somehow fails of doing so adequately, so that the
work of calming restoration has to be taken up by a more
divinely inspired and already by no means inexperienced
angel. But at least this introduction will be endeavouring,
with sincere intent, to prepare the way for the illumination
we may look to get from listening to the distinguished
Sabrinas and Michaels who are to come. But 'Hence with
denial vain, and coy excuse....'

Our perturbations about these last poems are likely to
begin with the title-page of our 1671 volume – to be seen
among the treasures of the University of Western Ontario's
Stuart Collection of Miltoniana. There *Paradise Regained*
is offered to us in a very emphatic typeface, while much
smaller, and perhaps hestitantly insignificant, type offers
the laconic information 'To which is added *Samson Agonistes*' – the provocative title of one of our lectures. We may
expect the problem of the relation between the two
poems to be raised not only there but incidentally on other
occasions. For what is involved is our reading of the moods
and bearings of the poems, and this interpretive problem,
inconclusively underlined by the title-page, has inevitably
involved differences of opinion about the mood or moods of
the later Milton, and these differences have involved other
complex differences of opinion about biographical details
and datings and poetic method and purpose and metrics.
The interpretive question is perhaps essentially about the
propriety of our being invited to pass from a poem representing the imperturbable resistance of the young Christ,
which makes possible the regaining of Paradise, to a poem
representing chiefly the perturbingly painful experience of
the defeated and enslaved Samson. Why should we be
invited to contemplate first the unswerving rectitude of a
hero whose spiritual triumph we must regard as a foregone
conclusion, and then the misery in failure of one of the
most fallible of Old-Testament national heroes? Is the
addition a lapse, a clumsy afterthought, a response to the

booksellers' desire for a sizable volume? Or does the collocation represent the imperfectly resolved conflict of the
later Miltonic moods which we can discern in the poetic
difficulties we encounter in the two pieces? Does not the
first poem express, or move towards the expression of,
the tuningly harmonious vision of spirituality towards
which Milton was always striving to make his way and
needed all the more after being diverted into national
revolutionary efforts and defeated in them? And does not
the second poem chiefly represent the painfully guilty
despair of defeat and the difficulty of struggling out of
that towards vision? Should not Samson's fallen, if ultimately, in some sense, rescued, experience rather precede
Christ's making possible the regaining of Paradise for all
mankind, following mere historical or at any rate testamentary chronology? Or is there some deep significance in
this apparently inept reversal? Can we interpret our poems
in a way which will demonstrate that, despite their differences in form and dominant mood, they are properly
sequential? Can we demonstrate that our first poem provides or develops a datum, of vision or what else, towards
which the hero of our second poem is represented as making his way? What is the nature of that Miltonic datum?
And, remembering the Miltonic formulae for the function
of poetry, can we discern in our first poem, despite our
automatic assumption of the young Christ's total infalli-
bility, any features and effects that in some sense corres-
pond to the allaying process that percedes the tuning, the
process that for the fallen Samson is painfully purgative
yet leads at last to some sort of resolution?

In short, are the two poems – as examinations have often
inquired and will no doubt often inquire again – to be
regarded as companion or rather as contrasting pieces? This
is a question that involves the contrasting relation and
difficult sequentiality of the two poems not only in their
Old and New (or rather New and Old) testamentary

materials but in their tone and mood, in their manipulation of apparently contrasting poetic forms in some yet related way, and in their representation of human experience (for the hero of our first poem is, after all, the Incarnate Christ) and of the varieties of possible response to it. And it is a question difficult to contemplate without some reference to the archetypal tragic pattern of Milton's experience and his poetic response to that, even if we take that pattern in the mythic large, disdaining the tangled pedantries of biographical and historical scholarship. For all critics, to a greater or less degree, recognize Miltonically experiential elements as involved in the universalizing process of our poems, in what Christ has to say of his early Miltonic education and in his response to the later Satanic temptation of learning, for instance, and of course especially in Samson's moving expression of defeated and blinded pain and in his contempt for his people for failing him.

Relevant or irrelevant as such facts of Miltonic experience may be to our aesthetic contemplation of our poems, the question of their relation is likely to be rendered the more perturbing when we turn the title-page of our volume and find *Paradise Regained* beginning by attaching itself, as in some sense a sequel, to *Paradise Lost* (I, 1–7):

> I who e're while the happy Garden sung,
> By one mans disobedience lost, now sing
> Recover'd Paradise to all mankind,
> By one mans firm obedience fully tri'd
> Through all temptation, and the Tempter foil'd
> In all his wiles, defeated and repuls't,
> And *Eden* rais'd in the wast Wilderness.

With its first and second Pauline echoes, this is a declaration which relates this poem, and so in some sense or other our volume, to all that our earlier poem has represented to to us of lost happiness and disobedience. We shall naturally try to understand the 'Recover'd Paradise' in terms of what was prefigured of it in the Paradise that was lost, though we may have to follow recent critics in recognizing that the original Paradise was not a place of merely placid security but presented challenging opportunities not well met by our first parents yet perhaps still to be responded to in the recovered state. And we shall undoubtedly accept what has become an accepted principle in commentary on our two poems: that each in its way assumes and rehandles the process of the Fall of Adam (and Eve), the one by representing an undeviating resistance to the Satanic temptation, the other by representing a more painful yet progressive resistance, after disastrous fall, to a repetition of earlier temptations. In some sense we are involved with the last two items in a trilogy, rather than merely with a pair of companion or contrasting pieces; and we shall not wish to deprive ourselves of the dividend to be derived from a third point of reference, though even what we have just noted clearly involves some perturbing interpretative complexities. But this will serve to remind us that we have a point of reference in *Paradise Lost*, in the experience, both purgative and restorative, through which Adam is led by Michael in the last two books of the earlier epic. (Properly speaking, for 1671, the last book — though heaven forbid that we should here get ourselves involved in the question of what Milton was trying to do by the new divisions yet to come: we must content ourselves with speaking of the last two books as we now read them in their emphatic division.) It has often been felt that in our two poems Milton was rehearsing yet twice more the pattern of those last two books. And it has sometimes been suggested that he did so because he himself felt the dissatisfaction with them expressed by many critics. If so, the fact at least testifies to the crucial importance that pattern held for him. And that more than justifies our appreciative interest in the reconsiderations of these last books by so many critics of late. It used to be the prevailing inclination to regard those last two books as sharply opposed, as our two poems have sometimes, at least at first sight, been thought to be. In this sense, the second-last book of *Paradise Lost*, with its terrible vision of history as the record of sinfully worldly human corruption as a result of the Fall, may seem to be, for Adam and for us, only painfully purgative. And the last book, with its account of prophetically angry and isolated just men leading forward to the prophecy of Redemption, forward from the Old Testament to the New, may seem an exhortation to a re-pudiatory and other-worldly faith providing restorative spiritual rescue, certainty, and compensation – if that is what we are to believe the later, dehumanized Milton had come to think the New Testament and Christianity to be all about. But recent commentators on these last books – among whom are to be numbered in one way or another all the lecturers in our series – have been leading us to discern that their matter is not merely a matter of such simple contrast, between purgation and restoration, the worldly and the other-worldly, the painful and the transporting, the corrupted natural and the transcendentally spiritual. There is continuity as well as contrast between the stages of Adam's progressive experience in the eleventh and twelfth books; and we find ourselves increasingly interested in and perplexed by the process of this progressive experience, and thus with what it is that Adam carried with him, in faith, into Eden and thus indeed into all the world. We may carry this interest and perplexity with us into our reading of our two poems, with the stimulus of our lecturers. We may begin by supposing that *Paradise Regained* is chiefly concerned with purely spiritual restoration, and that *Samson Ago-nistes* is chiefly concerned with painful purgation, that our first poem echoes our last book and our second echoes our second last. But we are not likely, under Milton's poetic right hand, to be able to maintain that or any other simpli-fication for long. We shall find ourselves confronted, all the more so with *Paradise Lost* behind us, with the sorts of

questions posed earlier; and perhaps not least with the
question as to what is continuously involved in these
representations of a process of experience somehow including and relating purgation and allaying and tempering and
tuning. And tuning for what?

Even our introductory link between our first poem and
Paradise Lost suggests such questions, despite its apparent
simplicity of statement, and its apparently simple contrasts,
if we read it with the intentness variously illustrated by the
commentaries of our lecturers and with the sensitive awareness of echoes taught us especially by Professor Rajan. The
'one mans firm obedience' must carry us back to what
Adam has learned by the end of his twelfth book, when he
says that henceforth he learns that to obey is best, having
been taught this by the example of the Redeemer – whose
exemplary as well as redemptive function is perhaps being
further illustrated in *Paradise Regained*. 'Obedience' is not
for Milton a simple word; and it is not easy to believe that
even the later Milton thought of it as implying mere submission, even a mere submission to purgative misery in the
hope of some otherwise unmerited reward in compensation,
though something of that may be dominant in Adam's
statement. To which, however, is added by Michael the
exhortation, 'onely add Deeds to thy knowledge answerable. ...' What sort of deeds? To what sort of deeds does the
now fully mature Christ proceed, after his obedient preparation through obedient resistance to the perversions of
Satanic temptation, when he returns from the waste wilderness to the world of men? And how are we to relate to such
deeds the deeds with which our desperately fallen Old-
Testament hero heroically finishes a life heroic? And how
do such deeds spring from and produce the calm of mind we
look for – the calm of mind promised Adam as the reward
of such deeds, in a now badly worn phrase? And perhaps
above all – since we are perforce chiefly concerned today
with perturbations, with a view to allaying, if not purga-

tion, to come – what do such deeds demand as to the spending of passion?

These are some of the questions initially invited by our poems, and already clarified and illuminated by our lecturers in their previously published commentaries.[6] With such questions in mind, we may now find it useful to review our poems briefly, in order to illustrate our questions further and especially to prepare ourselves for the further clarification and illumination to come.

By attaching itself in its opening lines, as in some sense a sequel, to *Paradise Lost*, *Paradise Regained* offers itself to us as a brief epic, to be interpreted in terms of its manipulation of the epic conventions of the earlier poem. But its epic effects – of councils, cosmic flights, harangues, similes, and so forth – have always seemed to critics strangely incidental and subordinate. There is little of the epic sweep of the earlier poem; instead our attention is concentrated on the debate in the wilderness, Christianizing the themes of such trials as Job's and echoing in some measure the trials of such as Hercules. Professor Lewalski's massive account of the brief-epic genre and of Milton's art in handling it should have invalidated an impression that used to be

6 It will be obvious that the inquiries in the preceding pages, and the suggestions occurring in the brief reviews to follow, have been particularly stimulated by the following: Professor Rajan's *The Lofty Rhyme: A Study of Milton's Major Poetry* (London 1970); especially its consideration of 'The Web of Responsibility,' 'The Hill of History,' and 'The Providence of Style' in *Paradise Lost*, and of 'Jerusalem and Athens' and 'The Unsearchable Dispose' in the poems of 1671; 'The Style of *Paradise Lost*,' in *Milton's Epic Poetry*, edited by C.A. Patrides; (Harmondsworth 1967); '*Paradise Lost*' and the *Seventeenth Century Reader* (London 1947); 'Simple, Sensuous, and Passionate,' in *The Review of English Study*, XXI (1945), 289–301, reprinted in *Milton: Modern Essays in Criticism* (New York 1965); '*Paradise Lost*: The Critic and the Historian,' *University of Windsor Review*, I (1965), 42–50; Professor Lewalski's 'Milton on Learning and the Learned-Minister Controversy,' in *HLQ*, XXIV (1961), 267–81; 'Innocence and Experience in Milton's Eden,' in *New Essays on 'Paradise Lost'* edited by T. Kranidas (Berkeley 1969); 'Structure and the Symbolism of Vision in

prevalent – that the later epic's failure as epic is symptomatic of despairing failure in Milton himself. With the help of many critics, we have come to see that the incidental manipulation of epic effects may be regarded as purposeful, in a way already recognizable in some degree in the manipulation of the larger epic effects of the early books of *Paradise Lost* and their incidental effect in the later ones: it provides an impressive universalizing frame, but it focuses our attention on the debate and on the processes of mind of the antagonists. It is with the implications of the debate and of those processes of mind that interpretative criticism is currently concerned.

It is because of this problem of genre, associated with the despair of the later Milton, that the critical tradition until lately uniformly tended to regard *Paradise Regained*, and *Samson Agonistes* with it, as vastly inferior to the heroic achievement of the earlier epic, however lamely

Michael's Prophecy, *Paradise Lost*, Books xi–xii,' in *PQ*, xlii (1963), 25–35; 'Theme and Structure in *Paradise Regained*,' in *Milton's Epic Poetry*, edited by C.A. Patrides; *Milton's Brief Epic: The Genre, Meaning, and Art of 'Paradise Regained'* (Providence 1966); 'The Ship-Tempest Imagery in *Samson Agonistes*,' *Notes and Queries*, N.S.6 (1959), 372–3; Professor Samuel's *Plato and Milton* (Ithaca 1947); *Dante and Milton: 'The Commedia' and 'Paradise Lost'* (Ithaca 1966); '*Paradise Lost*' in *Critical Approaches to Six Major English Works*, edited by R.M. Lumiansky and H. Baker (Philadelphia 1968); 'The Dialogue in Heaven: A Reconsideration of *Paradise Lost*, iii, 1–417,' in *PMLA*, lxxii (1957), 601–11, and reprinted, with revisions, in *Milton: Modern Essays in Criticism*; 'Milton on Learning and Wisdom,' in *PMLA*, lxiv (1949), 708–23; 'Milton on Style,' *The Cornell Library Journal*, no.9 (Autumn 1969), 39–58; Professor Frye's *The Return of Eden: Five Essays on Milton's Epics* (Toronto 1965); 'The Revelation to Eve,' in '*Paradise Lost'*: *A Tercentenary Tribute*, edited by B. Rajan (Toronto 1969); 'The Typology of *Paradise Regained*,' in *MP*, liii (1956), 227–38, reprinted in *Milton: Modern Essays in Criticism*, and in *Milton's Epic Poetry*, edited by C.A. Patrides, and revised in *The Return of Eden*; 'Notes on the Tragic Hero,' excerpted from *Anatomy of Criticism* in *Twentieth Century Interpretations of 'Samson Agonistes*,' edited by G.M. Crump (Englewood Cliffs 1968).

finished it itself was. Critical concern with the last two books of *Paradise Lost* and with the two succeeding poems has been significantly reversing a trend. There are many surprised reports in the eighteenth century of Milton's perverse annoyance at hearing the obviously superior and largely neo-classical epic preferred to the obviously inferior and (neo-classically) unheroic sequel. There is even one strange report, in an obscure eighteenth-century periodical, that *Paradise Regained* is unfinished – an assertion that has sometimes been made more elaborately about *Samson Agonistes* by modern scholarship. We hear little of the apparently unheroic sequel in the nineteenth century, even from the pious. Perhaps even they were inclined to feel with some of our older critics what we indeed may be much inclined to feel at this introductory stage in our response: that the inadequately epic effects and the tensions of response to temptation underscore the repudiatory preoccupations of *Paradise Regained* and render it a poem of the restrictive, and indeed unregenerately Puritanical, virtues, and even that we are watching a frustratedly agonized Milton tragically tearing out the very heart of the heroic humanistic values that motivated, or unhappily mismotivated, so much of his revolutionary prose. Most recent commentary on the poem has been concerned to offset these older undervaluations by demonstrating that *Paradise Regained* is, even through its apparent negatives, a representation of heroically spiritual virtues, an endeavour which of course involves us in deciding what we think are the character and implications of such virtues for Milton (and, so far as they may be relevant, for ourselves).

Perceptive critics, including our lecturers, have led us to recognize that what is crucial in the poem is what Satan is trying for his own protection to find out: the meaning of the baptismal divine declaration that Christ is the Son of God. And they have carried us beyond the Satanic form of the question, posed in temptations that used to seem and for some still seem the main burden of the poem. We have come to recognize that the main burden of the poem is the progressive discovery by the Christ, who is at that point passing from youth to maturity, of the meaning of that declaration for him. He is, our critics have made clear, discovering the character of his mediatorial office and what it implies for himself and for men. Satan's attempt is to discover the meaning of this office, and to pervert it, by the three temptations which seem to provide the poem with its structure. First there is the temptation to turn the wilderness stones into bread, so that Christ may feed both his hungering self and other poorer souls starving in the wilderness. Last (and with a significant preference for one gospel's order to the other's), there is the climactic temptation of the temple's pinnacle. And in the middle there is the impressive elaboration of the temptations of the kingdoms of this world which makes of central significance Christ's resistance to Satanic perversions of those values and means which so much dominated the consciousness of Milton's late-Renaissance age: wealth and power, glory, national zeal and victory over enemies, and finally learning or knowledge or *scientia*. Commentary used habitually to deplore the apparently negative preoccupation of Milton's Christ with mere resistance to temptation. And many readers are still apt to be impressed chiefly by the detached coldness of the Miltonic Christ. But we now see the poem as the representation of a temporarily withdrawn contemplative combat, representing, through the repudiations of Satanic perversities, the achievement of the spiritual triumph celebrated by the poem's concluding angelic chorus – a triumph which adumbrates and prefigures the triumphs to come. The poem is challenging us to recognize what those triumphs require of Christ as Mediator. But, since the mediatorial office is also, in its very process, exemplary, the poem seems also to be challenging us to recognize what men have to do to be saved, what effort of imitation is required of them.

The first temptation, we have been taught to see, is essentially a temptation to a failure of faith in the apparently severe divine providence that has led Christ, symbolically though also really hungering, into the wilderness of human suffering under sin and wrath. It is a situation which suggests not so much withdrawal from the world for pure contemplation as a confrontation with what is most painful in the human situation. It may remind us that the Incarnation is itself a sacrifice, as the opening verses of Milton's early Nativity poem say, or as we see, with Professor Samuel's help, from the Son's response to the apparently harsh Father's challenge in the third book of *Paradise Lost*. In response to the Satanic formulation of the challenge in terms of human misery, Milton's Christ asks the sharply positive question, 'Why dost thou then suggest to me distrust ...?' (I, 355). The rigid sharpness of the question is likely to be underlined for us in its Miltonic severity by the fact that it involves the rejection of the Satanic humanitarian appeal for the feeding of others in the wilderness. Perhaps we are required to remember at this point that we are in the initial stages of a process of developing discriminations that are not as easy, even for the young Christ to make, as we would like to assume; and no doubt we should recall – what we know and what the young Christ is in process of finding out – that the process will issue in a ministry in which thousands are fed. But at the moment, as our critics have taught us, the refusal of pervertedly Satanic motivation, and the echoing and anticipatory comment on mere bread alone, assert Christ's faith in and dependence on divine providence, his trusting acceptance of whatever apparently Satanic time and the mysteriously challenging will of heaven may lead him to. We may see this as the basic obedience which is perhaps, after fear, the lever of the Satanic appeal, the beginning of spiritual wisdom.

The elaborate second temptation – a temptation of the Satanically perverted values of the kingdoms of this world, not of the values of this world as it remains, however pollutedly, under the creative divine providence – then becomes a yet more insistent temptation to distrust. Satan invites Christ to depend, in the performance of his mediatorial, ministerial, exemplary office, on what the humanistic Renaissance mind, with its classical, indeed paganizing and modernizing, proclivities, regarded as the principal staffs of life. Christ's consistently firm, indeed increasingly contemptuous and severe, repudiation of these broken reeds, in favour of superior supports, demonstrates not only the continuance but the confirming and deepening of his trust. But it also demonstrates his increasing understanding of and confidence in his mission and himself. The climax of this part of the process is reached with what we are naturally inclined to regard as the most crucial of issues, for the Renaissance, Milton, and in modernized terms ourselves – the temptation to turn from repudiated wealth, power, glory, and so on, to find support or at least consolation in the merely human learning represented by the Satanic reading of the pagan classics. But, we are taught, Milton's Christ, with Milton's experience behind him and the new Miltonic acquists of blindness, and revolutionary defeat, is well aware that this would prove only another form of unspiritualized distrust. He meets the eloquently persuasive Satanic offer of a worldly wisdom without faith with an eloquent expression of the sense – which has been founded in his earlier intent study of the literature and learning of his people – of the faith sustained by the prophetic Biblical tradition. He himself, of course, is in process of recognizing in what sense he is the fulfillment of that prophetic and typological tradition, as Professor Frye and Professor Lewalski, among many others, have explained to us. And here, of course, is the real issue in the poem, for Milton and his seventeenth-century readers, and (so far as it is relevant) for us. What is the character of that fulfillment? What did it mean for Milton? And what may it mean for us?

It is because of the crucial importance of this question to our response to the poem that the problem of classical and humanistic learning and its contrast with or relation to faith has been the topic of such illuminating commentary by all our critics, not least our lecturers, and not least among them Professor Samuel in a highly relevant article promising further wise comment to come. Clearly we need to be – and perhaps the poem has been thus built up to challenge us to be – as sensitively discriminating as we can about it. For our response to it will very strongly condition our response to the poem's conclusion and what it leads on to and implies.

The repudiation of Satanic paganism and the spirituality of the assertion about the literature of the Hebrews reduce Satan (as our critics justly agree in pointing out) to frustratedly violent anger, expressed in a futilely violent storm and in the final temptation. The storm is a wild effort to induce perturbation in Christ, such perturbation as all the Satanic temptations have been designed to induce for the undermining of Christ's trust and faith, such perturbations as Satan has always managed to induce in greater or less degree in all human beings since the Fall. But the Incarnate Son of God proves wholly imperturbable. In that he is exceptional, but perhaps also a fulfillment and an exemplar. And he remains so in response to Satan's climactic effort to perturb, to challenge Christ's trust, in what Satan thinks the desperately irresolvable dilemma of the temptation of the pinnacle. It is the pinnacle of the Old Testament temple, of course, representing the height to which the old dispensation could move, though to give place to the new. And it is perhaps, as some critics have suggested, for Milton a Gothic spire, though as yet without a crowning sign. Satan thinks that Christ must either stand there by himself self-balanced, which is in Satan's view impossible, or cast himself testingly down, depending on God to rescue him. Our critics rightly concentrate our attention not only on the wonder but on the complex implications of Christ's re-

sponse and the words in which it is expressed; and with
them we shall need to contemplate with care the ambiguity
or ambivalence or whatever it is of what is certainly in
every sense of the word a crux. 'Tempt not the Lord thy
God, he said and stood' (IV, 561). It is indeed a difficult
saying. It seems not only to reassert once more Christ's
obediently faithful trust in God but also his trust in himself.
Clearly he has come to recognize fully the implications of
his Incarnate Sonship; and many critics have read the statement as a now justifiable assertion of his own divinity, of
the God that is in him, and some have argued that in the
temptations it is only his human nature that is negatively
tried – there is a long theological tradition behind this – in
order that his pure divinity may at last be thus asserted for
miraculously saving purposes. Yet it is, as the poem's
indications of the context of the temptations keeps reminding us, the Incarnate Son who is being born into maturity,
and clearly the wonder is that he stands on the crucial
pinnacle in the human nature which incarnates his divinity.
And clearly Satan at last recognizes what it means to be
the humanly incarnate Son of God. Earlier in the poem he
has angrily asserted that he also is a son of God, or was.
Perhaps he now gets the applicable point that is being
finally made for him, and for us. 'But Satan smitten with
amazement fell ...'; and so on into the conclusive angelic
celebration of a preliminary victory which enables Christ to
perform, in later actions involving his humanity and divinity, his offices of mediator and exemplar. He is of course
passing onward to the ministry recorded in the Gospels:
'on thy glorious work Now enter, and begin to save mankind,' the angels somewhat inconclusively, for the time
being, conclude. And 'hee unobserv'd Home to his Mothers
house private return'd.' Unobserved and private as yet, we
may be induced to add, looking forward to the ministry and
the actions of a divinely supported humanity for which the
process represented in this poem has been preparatory.

Despite its brevity, that review should have focussed our attention on some of the problems to be considered in our further consideration of the poem, and it may have suggested some principles worth bearing in mind. Most of these are connected with a misleading inclination reflected by the review itself: it tended to follow the pattern provided by the Satanic temptations, as if that were the structural pattern of the poem, as if the Satanic controlled the poem, the situation, the shape of the process, as we are only too prone to think it controls the human situation, the shape of the process of history, and indeed the world. But that is the basic Satanic delusion and illusion: once accepted, it leads into the perturbation, the distrust, the failure of faith, the despairing leaps this way or that, to which Christ cannot be induced – and to which he and the poem are perhaps going on to try to teach men, yet further than in the past, how not to be induced. Though he is imperturbable, we may note, in this connection and in connection with the question about purgation we raised earlier, that he has to learn and know what these traps are. And we may recall, what the poem does not allow us to forget, that he will come close to despair on a later, crucially climactic occasion. What controls the poem then? In considering its manipulation of its genre, we may profitably reflect on what Professor Rajan has written recently in reconsidering the sometimes supposedly highly balanced pattern of Milton's earlier Nativity ode, of the asymmetrical effects to be discerned in that poem by more sensitive readers. Milton, we perceive thence, habitually works thus. If *Lycidas* has a balanced structure, what are we to say of its prevailing rhyme-scheme – if it has one? These are perceptions worth application to the later poems. But simplemindedness may at least observe of our poem that it is Satan who is, to put it mildly, asymmetrical in it, and we should not allow ourselves to be taken in by the appearance of symmetry his sequence of temptations, with their overblown middle, presents. There is an

alternative symmetry, potentially self-balanced, that is in
process of being developed in the poem, though it is difficult
to apprehend its complex character. Perhaps the curiously
incidental manipulations of the conventions of the poem's
genre may suggest that this is what both God in his epic
heaven and Christ's human associates at home are waiting
for. At any rate, it may be worth repeating, in connection
with this matter of genre and structure and their manipulation, a vague suggestion made some years ago. The title-
page of our volume does at least emphatically present
Paradise Regained as a poem 'In iv Books.' Satan knows no
such four books – of any kind. His temptations spill across
the books in a confusion that makes us wonder whether
Milton knows, in this case as in others, what he is doing
with his divisions. Perhaps the arrangement of materials in
the books has contextual and developing significance. At
any rate, it might prove rewarding to look at what is concentrated on at the ends of the successive books. Despite
the Satanic asymmetry, they may be found to represent
stages in the process whereby Christ is confirming what he
has learned and indeed has always known, and is developing his sense of what that implies as to what is required of
him. For this dynamically self-balancing, though God-
trusting, process, the Satanic process is only an occasion, to
be submitted to, though not without some not unjustifiable
coldness and irritation with regard to the self-deluded
deluder.

And some such reflections as these may help us with the
cruxes we have noted in the poem, including the crux of
learning and its relation to faith. Nothing that Satan can
offer can be of value; but that is because Satan has nothing
to offer but what he himself has always striven to pervert
and has already perverted. But evil for Milton, as we can
discern from *Paradise Lost* and even from his prose, is
essentially the perversion of some good. Behind all Satan's
offers, with their delusions, lie goods that were created for

man's use and for the man-God's use, not excluding either
bread or learning. As to learning, Satan is not offering
the classical tradition at its best; he is offering the Satanic
perversion of it, which is all he knows and which he
himself has induced through distrustful perturbations
springing from himself when his influence is not resisted.
We are not being required, as we are inclined in our perturbation to think, to reject some evil or worldly thing in favour
of some wholly supernal good. The discrimination – if we
dare use the word these days – is not between earthly
black and heavenly white: it is rather between a perverted
misuse and a creatively right use. We are watching the
maturing Christ confirming such discriminations as the
basis for what he will say and do in a ministry which, or so
St Paul thought, removed the wall of partition between
good pagan and good Hebrew. And we are doing so in a
poem which, as we already well know, does not repudiate
the learning and devices of the classical tradition but makes
good use of them, as of the Old Testament, for the
humanely Christian purpose of allaying the perturbations
of the mind and inducing the affections to set themselves
in right tune.

We have already raised the question of the extent to
which our other poem is to be regarded, in the terms of its
preface, as repeating or somehow contrastingly modifying
this purpose through purging and tempering. And whether
we end by regarding *Samson Agonistes* as a contrasting
rather than a companion piece, or as a companion rather
than a contrasting piece, or as in some significant sense the
one because in some degree the other, the same sorts of
questions will present themselves with respect to it. There
is again the problem of poetic genre and the manipulation
of it. And this at once presents the problem of the
Miltonic relation or tension between the Classical and
Biblical, and between the humanistic and the religious. And
– though a superficial annotator may testify that this poem

appears to present fewer allusive problems than most of Milton's other poems – this carries with it the problem of Milton's later response to learning, of what he is doing with his learning, of what view of learning and of the Classical tradition the poem is communicating to us, of whether it is to be in the end repudiated or regarded as somehow instrumental. Since the hero of *Samson Agonistes* is obviously far from notably learned, whereas the hero of *Paradise Regained* quite as obviously is, this will present us with the question as to what Milton supposed the Old-Testament hero and his fellows might be assumed to know, or to have had the opportunity of knowing and of using in their response to experience. That will reintroduce the question of the relation between, or the contrast between, the Classical or humanistic and the Biblical tradition; and of course that will bring with it a question – clearly central to the process of comprehension represented by our other poem – of the relation, or contrast, between the Old Testament and the New. Among other matters, this is likely to involve us in the question about the manner in which Samson and his Old Testament fellows, and their poem, succeed in justifying the ways of God to men – clearly a basic matter underlying all we have been saying, and one we must ultimately contemplate in Miltonic terms, whether we regard our poems as companion sequels to Milton's earlier epic effort or not. And that question carries with it, at any rate for Milton, the question of the character of the response required of just men to God's ways, whatever they are, and of the relation or contrast between the responses required under the old dispensation and under the new. This raises the question of Milton's reading of Old Testament typology, of his handling in our poem of the principle by which Old Testament just men are regarded as witnesses by their prefiguration of Christ and what Christ implies. The Christ of *Paradise Regained* is evidently in some degree to be regarded as in process of recognizing fully, in terms of contrasting Satanic perversions and the cumulative insights and examples among his people, and in terms of what he is now called on to do, what is required of him in fulfillment of this prefiguration, what it is to be a fully just man in the human condition (and so what it is to be the Son of God, or – what Satan and his like are not, a son of God). Thus we may find ourselves driven to ask what our poem is attempting to tell us in answer to the question, What is a just man? – a question as to which even Pontius Pilate did not, in his perturbing perplexity, stay for an answer. Perhaps that question would have been, and is, irrelevant. In some sense, it appears to have become so for many sorts of people professing themselves Christians in Milton's day, especially in the face of what they thought the disastrous collapse not only of Christendom but of civilization and indeed of the human race in a history near its final doom. Their inclination was to look for release from their perturbations by believing that the imperfect Old Testament types had been finally and once and for all fulfilled in the Incarnate Son, and that that was that; that in him and by his actions a truth – to go back to Bacon's Pilatical word – had been finally revealed in which they had only to have faith in order to be saved, without any works of theirs – just or otherwise, and meanwhile to be compensatingly sustained in a disastrously Satanic world. If we are not careful, we are now likely to find ourselves getting involved in the complexities of seventeenth-century theology and of the Milton theological response to this ancient problem of merit in terms of faith or works or both – a topic intently canvassed by many students and critics of Milton, not least by Professor Rajan in his recent explication of Milton's lofty rhyme, and by Miss Samuel in her concern to demonstrate that the Platonic ethic is of continuous relevance for Milton, or to persuade us that something related to this is being exemplified by the Son in *Paradise Lost* and that

that poem is essentially an ethically educational poem. But we must not, now, stay for such recondite, and, as many are inclined to think, such unpoetical and unaesthetic questions. Yet we do need at least to bear in mind this paradisally-lost Miltonic question of the just man in an unjust world. If we do not, we may find ourselves running the risk of concluding that not only Milton's theology but his poetry is in the end irrelevant – that his works are as irrelevant to our condition as his faith must be admitted to be to most, even after we have attempted to translate it into modernized aesthetic terms in the hope that these at least will prove viable among a fit audience of a few just critics, like ourselves. And unhappily, we are likely to find that critical operation more difficult to conduct with Samson than with our other hero. What justice, what humanity, what Christianity, can be discerned in the terrible catastrophe of Samson's play?

That may be the question as to which we find ourselves most looking for illumination to come, as it is perhaps the question lying behind the questions we have so far raised about this poem and behind the wide variety of critical responses to it.

The problem of genre is presented to us at once by Milton's preface to the drama. After rephrasing the classical notion of the function of drama into the purgative and tempering – and, we should note, after connecting this notion, through a reference to St Paul, with the tragic pattern and function of the Book of Revelation, the preface goes on to justify and underline the poem's use of Greek tragic conventions. Indeed, it reproduces these in a way more strictly neo-classical than anything attempted by any single Greek, any doctrinaire Renaissance humanist, or any eighteenth-century rhymer. In doing so, it relentlessly concentrates our attention on the painfully defeated and wretchedly guilty isolation of the tragic hero, for at least two-thirds of its course perhaps, and then, somewhat suddenly we feel, on such an abrupt change of direction as the Greeks were fond of and had a word for – though in this tragedy the change is of a somewhat unGreek character we shall have to account for. In this conventional concentration, the poem must seem to be underscoring something like the sense of inevitable fatality we associate with Greek tragedy and its view of the human situation; and that impression is certainly sustained by most of what is said by our hero and his associates. It is evidently even possible to believe that this is all that classicism and humanism, through frustrating experience, have left for Milton.

But on the other hand some of our older critics were so much impressed by the oppressively negative implications that seemed to them to dominate the poem not only at its beginning but throughout that they felt its neo-classical rigidities chiefly served to throw into relief the terrible and wrathful rigidities they supposed him to find in his Hebraic materials, as a consequence of the intensified rigidities of his Puritan temper under defeat. (What sort of dilemma we get ourselves into by describing the author of *Areopagitica*, with its Samsonesque overtones, as a Puritan, we must certainly not stay to ask: we shall only be told that *Areopagitica* is irrelevant to 1671, and that Milton the revolutionary was confusedly more of a Puritan than anything else in any case, and that he became even more so in some way after the defeat of the Puritanism the confused other part of him attacks in *Areopagitica*.) Certainly our poem is remarkably consistent, despite its classical genre and tone, in keeping the decorum of its Hebraic time – though some critics have complained that it does not adequately reproduce the crudities to be associated with the Paul Bunyanesque folk-hero of the Book of Judges and so, presumably in their opinion, does not adequately represent the way in which he was near-orientally mythologized. But we can readily understand why our poem has sometimes been said to be unredeemedly Hebraic in its bearing, because it seems

chiefly occupied with the harsh retribution meted out by
the wrathful Old Testament deity to his failed heroes as
well as to his enemies, with the harshness already charac-
terized by the brutally self-justifying God of the third book
of *Paradise Lost*. And with a wrathful harshness such as it
is difficult for us to believe the defeated Milton did not wish
he could implement against all his enemies. This, by the by,
has induced some readers, especially of a Whiggish persuasion, to deem the poem a further call to arms in liberties
defence, which anticipated and contributed to the coming
revolution of 1688–9 (which however providentially proved
bloodless). And perhaps, if we are good enough salesmen
we might sell it even now as a relevant tract for the times.
But this simply fatalistic reading of the poem does not
adequately satisfy us. It does have the virtue of at least
relating, instead of opposing, Milton's Hellenism and
Hebraism; but it does so by relating what is least sustaining
and most perturbing in both traditions, even for those of us
who think that that was what the defeated later Milton,
simply as a man when he was no son of the muses, was like.
Our critical efforts, rightly, seek a more poetical testament.

They do so, to begin with, by recognizing that, as is
always the case with him, Milton is not simply reproducing
but manipulating the humanist classical conventions with a
vengeance. If they carry with them the Hellenistic and
Hebraic sense of fatality, they do so in order to represent
the way in which Samson ultimately, as we say, transcends
this perturbing sense. And all the conventions are manipu-
lated in a way which concentrates our attention on the state
of Samson's affections, passions, mind, and soul. All critics
now agree in thinking Samuel Johnson mistaken in com-
plaining that our poem fails as a tragedy because it has no
middle, that its action is imperfect because nothing is done,
though much is suffered, between its beginning and end.
Dr Johnson was wrong in his notion of action, as perhaps
even Aristotle might have told him. The action in *Samson*

is, we say, a spiritual action. And we are confirmed in this not only by what we now see in the manipulation of conventions but by Milton's prefatory insistence that this drama was never intended for humanized representation on the stage. We see that it is a closet-drama, and we conclude that we are to read it in the isolation of our closets, as we think Milton wrote it in the blinded isolation of his closet, despairingly closing the door on all merely mundane and human relations, in favour of a transcendent spiritual and poetic relation to something immutably absolute. Thus we read the tragedy as a representation of the transfiguration of despairing isolation into the spiritualized isolation necessary to the relation with the transcendentally eternal which alone can provide compensation for pain and calm within, we think, or think the later Milton must, in his closet, have thought.

It is chiefly in some such terms as these that we find companionship between our two pieces, despite the contrasts between their imperturbable and painfully perturbed heroes. As the young Christ isolates himself in the wilderness of this world to engage in wholly interiorized and self-closeted meditation, so Samson, however unintelligent and uncontemplative, is forced by the wrath of his just God and the pains of enslaved defeat to withdraw into himself. As Christ meets a series of temptations by a series of cold repudiations, so Samson meets the series of his renewed temptations by a series of repudiations through which his despair is transformed into a cold anger which is the expression of the contempt for the world proper to his new spirituality and which issues in a decisive witness to God's just wrath against the world in a destructive casting down more theatrically impressive than Satan's. And in this, Samson is to be seen as indeed prefiguringly typing, though he does not know it, the agony of the isolated logos to come.

But we have already perceived that, whatever else the manipulation of brief-epic conventions does in our other poem, its Christ is not thus simply detached by his meditations in the wilderness from the world. Indeed, despite the opinion of very high authority, it seems possible to assert that in Milton's later poems nobody is isolated and without relation or out of relation, save Satan and those who follow his lead – which of course in some degree and much of the time includes all of us, in Milton's theological opinion. Many critics have variously noted of late that it is Satan who asserts that the mind is its own place. ... They say rightly, in one way or another, that Milton thinks it must be God's place. But we have to ask carefully what that means, in relation to a God who is, as Milton seems to think, essentially creative and whose relations to his creatures are never unprovidentially broken, whatever they may think in their more Satanic moods. And it is the Satan of *Paradise Regained* who insists, angrily, in insisting that he too is or was a son of God, that relation holds, a somewhat Satanically inadequate word. Of course nobody can doubt Milton's concern with the mind, and its affections and reflections: his dramatic manipulation of all conventions in the later, as in some degree in most of the earlier, poems concentrates our attention on the motivating processes of the mind, reflecting the dramatic tradition immediately preceding him. But the key is in motivation, not isolation, and in his concern with motivation to kinds of action. The manipulation of brief-epic conventions in our other poem does not, we have perceived, isolate the motivations Christ is contemplating from actions, from actions involving not only his sonship relation to God but the relations to others implicit in that. The manipulation of brief-epic conventions provides us with the context of the meditation, not simply through Satan's reminiscences of his past efforts and his presentation of the world, but through Christ's reflections on the past experience of men, both those within and those without the law, and by his developing anticipation of what is to come in the subsequent brief epic of the Gospels, for which

his mother and his associates are waiting and whose terms
are anticipatingly echoed and reechoed throughout the
texture of the poem, much more even than those of the
Book of Job or any other poem. Samson's thoughts are
similarly in large part reminiscential to begin with, and
they reflect, though in despair, the history and experience
of his people. Towards what do they make their way? Evidently we must indeed do very much better than Dr
Johnson in our discriminating appraisal of action. In doing
so, we shall need to reflect that the closet-drama we are to
imagine in process before us does not at all represent
Samson as at any point isolated. Even when he is at the mill,
he is with slaves. And, depending on how one imagines his
choral associates, the cast of his play includes upwards of
twenty-six speaking persons. Indeed, as Cecil B. De Mille
would say of such catastrophically theatrical ventures as
his own, it in some sense, by its reminiscences and anticipa-
tions much more than by its hordes of unseen Philistines,
involves a cast of thousands – in more Miltonic terms, a
cast of thousands and thousands in them who love God and
strive to keep his commandments. As the experience of
Christ temporarily isolated, with Satan, in the wilderness,
moves towards his ministerial relations with the world of
men, so the action of Samson's drama, beginning with his
isolation in despair, may be thought of as moving towards
the redirected reestablishment of his relations. Because of
the catastrophic theatricality of its conclusion, it is difficult
to avoid the implication that these redirected relations
concern only his spiritual relations with God, redirected by
the transfiguration of isolated despair into isolated other-
worldly spirituality – a process sustained by a series of
repudiations in response to renewed temptation, and rever-
beratingly confirmed by the conclusion of this heroic
revenge-tragedy. But this was a kind of response to experience that Hebrews felt themselves forced into throughout
their historical experience – not least when their own temple

was in due time destroyed. And we have noted that the inclination to such a response was naturally strong when the reformed Puritan temple was destroyed – without ever having had its foundations truly laid, let alone its pinnacle erected. Is it possible that *Samson Agonistes* is challenging Milton's contemporaries, and us, to ask whether this is in truth what hangs on all the Law and the prophets? Is it perhaps in some such sense as this that we are being invited to regard our two poems as contrasting yet somehow companion pieces? – though whether the first should be last or the last first may remain an insoluble question, and part of the challenge.

These at any rate would seem to be some of the questions worth our considering as we follow, with our lecturers, the action of our play. It may prove useful to consider it in terms of a five-act structure that some critics have seen in it, thrown into relief by Milton's manipulation of the classical conventions. These 'acts' are not specified by our text of course; and the effect is far from being justified by Greek tragic precedent: it is the result of Milton's neo-classical tendency to organize his poetic material in balanced blocks. And of course account has to be taken, or should be taken in more leisurely and sensitive explication, of the destructuring asymmetrical effects communicated by the flowing metrical and loftily rhyming patterns of heroic declamations and choral odes. But we are here involved only in an initial effort to render our material in some degree intelligible, so that we may recognize the problems, or challenges, it presents; and we must for the time being suspend many disbeliefs.

Certainly the 'five-act structure' seems at first to underscore the rigidities we associate with neo-classicism and Hebraism. It first presents Samson to us as isolated in his enslaved despair; it then, in three acts, presents him to us as resisting renewed temptations, in some sense through his increasingly despairing sense of guilt and the justice of a wrathful God's ways; and it concludes by telling of his triumphant revenge on his and his God's enemies. The question is about how he got from the beginning to his end, and what the process and the conclusion mean.

In the first 'act' Samson himself concentrates our attention on his enslaved – though already in some sense self-enslaved – condition, as he is released from his oppressively eyeless labours, into the sun for a moment, by the Philistine sun-god's holy day. He does so in some of the most pain-wracked lines in English poetry, impossible not to regard as issuing from the depths of the blind poet's own soul. And when the chorus of enslaved Hebrews approaches him, to complete this first act, their pity only serves, for him and for us, to exacerbate the torturing incisions of the sense of failure and guilt under a wrathful God.

Indeed, despite its pitying and better inclinations, this seems the principal function of the neo-classical chorus of enslaved and unredeemed Hebrews throughout, until it arrives on a sudden, in the end, at its liberated wonder at Samson's end. Its lamenting Old Testament uncertainties about the ways of its supposedly just but harshly retributive God, its efforts to suppress its own reasoning on such matters – at least what it suspects is its vain reasoning, its despairing assertion that the only alternatives its God and experience present are those of heroic action only too likely to fail or of repentantly martyred submission (which appears to it the only alternative open to Samson now), its terrified perturbations as the action moves through its penultimate challenges, all these seem chiefly to underscore Samson's tortured guilt and the fatal justice of his despairing sense of Heaven's desertion. And despite what we know of the limited percipience of the choral wailings of Greek old men and women, we are of course much inclined to follow the choral comment on Samson as our guide through this labyrinth, to regard its theological cruxes as, though old-testamentary and because so, representative of the theological preoccupations the later Milton discarded in favour of spiritualized poetic vision, and to find this conclusively expressed in the wonder of the final choral utterance, to provide the absolutely conclusive poetic statement we want Milton's poetry to give us — and are so much inclined to complain that it does not adequately give us because of his unresolved conflicts. Perhaps we need, without being totally unsympathetic to the Hebraic dilemma, to be a little more objective about the ongoing choral comments throughout, and even its wondering comments in the end, in terms of what these now-liberated Hebrews are going on to.

But, as the choral comments indicate for the chorus, the sense of guilt and fatality seems, at any rate at first, what not only the choral companions but Samson's successive visitants in the middle 'acts' chiefly impress upon him, despite his resistance to their various temptations — so that what we appear to be watching is an increasingly painful intensification of isolated perturbations which can be purged only by the transfiguration of guilty isolation into spiritualized isolation.

Yet some findings of recent scholarship and criticism may suggest the possibility that we are being challenged here, as with the apparent negatives of Christ's resistances to temptation, to attempt discriminations less simply paradoxical and transfiguring than we like. In the second 'act' the efforts of Samson's Hebrew father, Manoa, to persuade him to accept, in blinded defeat, the paternal endeavour to ransom him from the Philistines into the protective security of the Hebraic earthly home, seem to produce from Samson expressions of even more deeply self-embittered guilt and submission to God's harshly just ways. It is a sense deplored yet confirmed by the choral lamentations, and we seem only deeper in wretched isolation. A number of recent critics have stressed this by emphasizing Manoa's unenlightened stupidity in thinking that he can ransom Samson and that Samson's despair will induce him to accept such an escape. And with an eye to the inadequacies of the temporally oriented Hebraic notion of deliverance, the contrast is pointed up between the kind of ransom the fumbling Manoa offers and the kind of spiritual ransom, out of this world and into eternity, that is to come and of which Samson is to be thought to have in the end some mysterious revelation. Manoa is stupid; though he is hardly much more stupid than most fathers may be thought to be from either side of the generation gap. And his fumbling does underscore the gap between the perceptions of this generation of Jews and a later generation's. But it would be a pity to miss the fact of Manoa's concern; and it would be sad to imply that all an earthly father can do for his child is to persuade it, without fumbling, that there is nothing it can do but wait for spiritually isolating rescue by its heavenly father, if such there be, of whose concern an earthly father can provide no inkling. But there is something more to be made of the business than a defence of the well-intentioned stupidity of merely earthly fathers. Samson refuses ransom on the ground that he is guilty and does not merit it. We have already noted that many despairing seventeenth-century Christians looked for spiritual ransom, for rescuing redemption without any merit on their part, looked for another to foot entirely for them the redeeming bill; and before we leap up into pure spirituality from the Hebrew pinnacle, and assume that Milton now shares their expectation, we should perhaps consider the balance required and ask if Samson is not to be regarded as already in process of making it up, through the fulcrum of his despair and the tempering the sunshine and confrontations that may be working in him.

The third and central 'act' of course renews the temptation centric to Samson's final fall, with Delila, coming in full sail, like an overdressed ark royal, representing all the temptations of worldly flesh and its destruction of faith and obedience. It is clear enough what is represented by this somewhat restoration-comic figure, though the ironic presence of comic effects in the presentation of Samson's three principal visitants may perplex us, especially after Milton's prefatory notice of the indecorum of mixing crude comedy with tragedy. There are perhaps ironies of a not insignificant bearing still in his poetic process. But the response of the uneasy chorus gives us our lead here as usual, and we find decisive the renewed strength of Samson's resistance to renewed temptation in his diatribe – reminiscent of Greek and patristic and paradisally-lost denunciations of women. The diatribe seems by its violent negatives a repudiation of all that is embodied in this world's Eves, and this of course highly colours our sense of the mysteriously spiritualized renewal of Samson's strength and obedience and of what the chorus says of the compensating substitution of the visionary perceptions of the inner eye for the seductive deceits of the outward-looking eye, now happily blinded. Such implications are confirmed for us by the fact that Dalila is not simply represented as sexually seductive: under the circumstances, that might indeed have been somewhat absurdly indecorous. She is represented as offering Samson ransom, so that that theme, with all its attendant problems continues through this 'act' and goes on indeed through the rest of the drama. And she is represented as doing so through an apologetic defence of her Philistine patriotism. We may follow recent commentary in being curious about the function of that apologetic patriotism, especially since it echoes one of Satan's ploys in our other poem. Clearly an implication is that patriotism is not enough. And clearly Dalila's self-defence has the effect of throwing into relief, at least for us, if not for the chorus, the radical errors of Samson's earlier, self-centred and indeed egomaniacal patriotism – which have been his despairingly reminiscential concern throughout the action up to this point. But if evil in this world is a perversion and a parody of good, we shall perhaps need to inquire what sort of good in this world is being parodied by Dalila's patriotism and by Samson's earlier parodic version of national heroism. And if we say, as of course we are being inclined to by the drama, that what is required is a spiritual Patriotism, centred through our sonship to a heavenly father in our heavenly home, the assertion will bring with it the necessity of dealing with the question our drama may perhaps be beginning to seem all about: What sort of witness in the world is required by such sonship patriotism? And is the witness of merely despairing and repudiatory negativism and of visionary other-worldly spirituality enough – as so many souls in the seventeenth century tried to believe? In that connection we may find it profitable to consider something else about this central act that has been coming into the forefront of our awareness of late. It is not merely the repudiation of the perversely parodic that is underlined by the thunder of Samson's diatribe. The thunder throws into contrasting relief the restrained moderation of Samson's dismissal of Dalila. It is only too easy to trivialize such effects. But there would seem to be something to be said for the notion that the Miltonic thunders are all preliminary, and that we should not miss what comes through after what the thunder has said, in muted moments such as this one, and even in silences. At any rate, the muting at the end of the third act may suggest that what we have been watching throughout is not simply a process of purging by painful rejections but a tempering of passions.

It might prove worth our while to carry some such sense with us into the fourth 'act' where we have the two visitations of Harapha and the Messenger who brings the tidings of the Philistine demand that Samson perform at the Dagonish festival. Samson's reinvigorated response to the taunts of the Philistine braggart – one of the progeny of mere earthy giants – is heartening to us and the chorus, though something of his old gladiatorial heroics remains in this response. Yet because Samson is somehow providentially saved from faulty repetition by the essential cowardice of the parodic braggart, the encounter underscores not simply the renewal of strength but a renewed sense – sudden, it seems to us, but with emergent foreshadowings in what has preceded that may prove worth our meditation – that his strength was not and is not simply in the sunburst of his hair but in the living God. That that is not a simple matter issuing in simple resolutions is what is underscored by the crux presented by the Messenger's tidings in the second part of this fourth 'act' through Samson's initial refusal and the perturbations of the chorus. Those perturbations are, as perhaps always with the chorus, concerned with what is to be done in response to such a challenging situation by one who is under such strict requirements of the Law as Samson is under. The choral perturbation must carry us back into those complexities of obedience and performance we became involved in with our other poem; and it may prove worth our while to consider that the crux being presented to Samson and the chorus here is not unlike the crux Satan thinks he is presenting to Christ on the pinnacle of the Old Testament temple. But in considering those complexities and the possible resolutions of them, we should not allow ourselves to miss the surprising tone of Samson's response to the choral perturbations. As the Christ of *Paradise Regained* at a relatively early stage in its process has retorted to the Satanically parodic appeals of humanitarianism and patriotism by asking, in terms that greatly trouble us by their apparent coldness, what else the people but a herd confused, so Samson in his embittered despair has denounced his people, in the persons of the chorus, for their failure to respond to his earlier heroic efforts at rescue. But at the point in the drama we have now reached, the champion displays a surprising temper such as he has not displayed before and a temper that is thrown into relief by the temper expressed in his response to the braggart. In this double-scened 'act' we may find contrasting motifs being brought into some sort of difficult relation. For what Samson uncharacteristically expresses here, in surprisingly gentle phrases, and out of some sort of developing calm of mind in himself, is a sympathetic concern for the perturbed state of mind of the chorus that he has not shown before and that the phrases indicate we must think of him as carrying with him into the action he goes on to – an action involving in most perplexing ways not only retribution and self-liberation into spirituality but the historical as well as spiritual liberation of his people.

We must carry such considerations as these into our response to Samson's concluding act, though an introductory lecture must not presume to enter far into conclusions. But we should be prepared to find that the concluding act not only brings down the stones of the Philistine temple on the heads of God's enemies but brings down on our heads all the perturbing difficulties presented by the collapse of all temples to enforce whatever it is that Milton thinks is preferable for the upright heart and pure and whatever remains in that of his concern for the experience and practice of all that which is praiseworthy. Criticism has often been much inclined to feel that what Manoa thinks praiseworthy in Samson's quitting of himself chiefly reflects his paternal stupidity and self-inflation, and the temporally oriented preoccupations not only of Hebraism but of the Hellenistic humanism Milton has repudiated. But in what he has to say of celebrating poetry, Manoa is looking forward into the continuing process of that story, strewn with songs, to which the Christ of *Paradise Regained* is looking back in his developing perception of what lies before him. And, despite highly spiritualized asseverations, it is perhaps not yet entirely clear in what sense or to what degree the final choral comment is related to or requires us to reject or modify what Manoa says of Samson's witness. Of course we wish the chorus to finalize the business decisively for us; and that is evidently what it wants for itself. But, at the risk of seeming to be uncertain about the foundations of some aesthetically spiritualized pinnacles of perception, it may prove worth our asking whether or not the chorus is even yet fully aware that it has not reached finality but is involved in a perturbing continuum requiring the response of further painful tuning (1745–58).

> All is best, though we oft doubt,
> What th'unsearchable dispose
> Of highest wisdom brings about,
> And ever best found in the close.
> Oft he seems to hide his face,
> But unexpectedly returns
> And to his faithful Champion hath in place
> Bore witness gloriously; whence *Gaza* mourns
> And all that band them to resist
> His uncontroulable intent,
> His servants he with new acquist
> Of true experience from this great event
> With peace and consolation hath dismist,
> And calm of mind all passion spent.

Before we reduce the complex resonances of those final lines to some simple finality, we should remember that this remains a chorus of Hebrews, though now liberated, and contemplate what is involved in the perception of several recent critics that the resonances of Milton's manipulation of his materials and his poetic conventions keep reminding us that somehow this poem, especially in its collocation with its contrasting or companion piece, is presenting Samson to us not merely from the point of view of Old Testament Hebrews but also with reference to what was said to the progeny of our chorus in the later Epistle to the Hebrews.

The New Testament epistles look back to the Passion. *Paradise Regained* handles the temptations as dry run, in the wilderness, for the Passion. Samson's agony clearly fore-shadows the Passion. And if it is said that Milton never wrote directly about the Passion, save in one early poem justly regarded as execrable, that may be because it so much concerned him and because he was so much concerned with the difficulties in the way of a fully tuned response to it in his age. His age reflects a continuing pattern, still in some sense very much with us in our despairing frustration, with which the Epistle to the Hebrews, like other New Testament Epistles, strives to deal. To what extent is the liberated chorus aware of this, in its new acquist, as it makes its liberated way out of the Book of more-or-less Cromwellian judges and major-generals and into and through Kings, Chronicles, Job, the Psalms, Ecclesiastes and various lamentations, and the major and minor prophets, in the perturb-ing rhythm of its history, and so to the Epistle to the Hebrews, where Samson is briefly mentioned, among others in a cloud of witnesses? Like the other epistles, Hebrews is dealing with the apparent futility of the Passion for men in this world since Christ has failed to return to establish here his kingdom. We recall that the epistle assures its readers that his is a spiritual kingdom, that here they have no con-tinuing city, that the kingdom is in their hearts – though not in each separately despairing heart in its spiritualized isolation but in their hearts in their relations with each other through their relations with the Christ who has at least been there. Here, as in other epistles, they are told this in terms of the contrasting continuity of their covenant with the old covenant – whose ark has been the fatal bark whose torn rigging Samson may be thought of as striving to repair the ruins of, in witness, however darkly shadowed. If *Paradise Regained* can be thought of as leading into the Gospels, *Samson Agonistes* leads into the Epistles. And the pieces, for all their obvious contrast, may thus prove some-how companionable, if we can sufficiently suspend our dis-belief, and ask relevant questions and stay for answers that will prove more challengingly complex than simply resolutionary. For Samson may be seen to be leading into something not unrelated to what the angelic chorus of *Paradise Regained* is leading into; and this may be what the last chapter of the Epistle to the Hebrews is leading into in its comments on what Christianized Hebrews, surrounded by a cloud of remembered witnesses, are called on to do, as our New English Bible puts it, for one another while they are 'still in the world' in which they have an ever-present guide and so, as they are assured, need 'not be swept off your course by all sorts of outlandish teachers.' There is something more here than the mere consolation Samson's chorus looks to find: '... let us continually offer up to God the sacrifice of praise, and never forget to show kindness and to share what you have with others; for such are the sacrifices which God approves.'

But now we do seem to be descending from our mount of speculation into small trivialities – or shall seem to be doing so if we do not perceive that the complex resonances of Milton's poems may be designed to reinvigorate our response to such simplicities as despair is always obscuring, if we do not see that his poetic works are themselves deeds answerable, answerably motivated and designed, as he thought his God's ways were, to induce an answerable motivation, through which responsive readers might learn, in order to purge their minds of perturbations, how to tune their affections by the spending of passion for such purposes as bring some calm of mind. But this discourse can hardly presume to be answerable: it must be content to come in its very questionable shape to guide a little onward to what is to follow.

TIME AND HISTORY IN
PARADISE REGAINED

BARBARA LEWALSKI

𝕿he fact that conceptions of Time and History are
important to Milton's *Paradise Regained* has not gone
unnoticed by critics,[1] but we have not given due attention
to the complex ways in which these ideas contribute to the
development of the poem's thematic subtleties, advance its
dramatic action, and assist in the characterization of the
principal personages. An important structural element in
the poem, and the source of a good deal of its dramatic
tension, is the juxtaposition and confrontation of various
perspectives – the Father's, Satan's, Christ's – on Time and
History.

In his *Christian Doctrine* Milton defined time in abstract
Aristotelian terms as the measure of motion, but his poetic

1 See Arnold Stein, *Heroic Knowledge* (Minneapolis 1957), 3–134;
   Barbara K. Lewalski, *Milton's Brief Epic* (Providence, RI and
   London 1966), 256–65; Jackson Cope, 'Time and Space as Miltonic
   Symbol,' *ELH*, XXVI (1959), 497–513; Laurie Zwicky, '*Kairos* in
   Paradise Regained: The Divine Plan,' *ELH*, XXXI (1964), 271–7.

uses of it emphasize a speaker's or character's sense of or experience of the temporal order – either as a particular moment or occasion (*kairos*) or as the ongoing sequence of minutes, years, or events. For Milton's idea of history his unfinished *History of Britain* is suggestive, since it engages directly with questions of historical cause and historical pattern. Milton notes, for example, certain remarkable parallels between the failures, accidents, and conquests suffered by the early Britons and such events in his own time, and attributes such recurrences ultimately to the Providence of God who 'after 12 ages and more had drawne so near a parallel betweene their state and ours in the late commotions.'[2] In *Paradise Regained* the characters' perceptions of and experiences of time are of central significance, as are also their philosophies of history – their various interpretations of the temptation episode in relation to past and future events and according to the categories of causality and pattern.

In his single speech in the introduction to Book 1 (130–72)[3] the Father provides authoritative terms of reference for the other views presented. 'Smiling,' confident, and without anxiety, he here invites Gabriel and the other angels to watch the momentous combat of wit and words about to take place. God's divine perspective affords transcendence of the uncertainties of time and chance, but not because of a sharp disjunction between man's time and God's eternity. Indeed, God's language in this passage dwells persistently upon the temporal categories of past, present, future: 'This man born and now up-grown,/ ... henceforth I expose/ To Satan'; 'He now shall know I can produce a man/ ... far abler'; 'But first I mean/ To exercise him in the Wilderness,/ ... e're I send him forth'; 'They now, and men hereafter.' Although this language may be

2 *The History of Britain,* in *The Works of John Milton,* 18 vols., ed. F.A. Patterson et al. (New York 1932–8), x, 317. Subsequent references to Milton's prose works are to this Columbia edition.
3 All references to Milton's poetry are to the Columbia edition.

explained by the epic convention which dictates the presentation of God as a kind of Zeus figure, or by the theological principle of accommodation whereby God is understood to present himself in terms suited to human conceptions, there is a basis in Milton's *Christian Doctrine* for supposing that he seriously intends the implication that perceptions of time on earth and in heaven are more alike than on earth is thought. As C.A. Patrides has noted,[4] Milton departs sharply from the theological commonplace linking the beginning of time to the creation of the world. Augustine had declared that 'the world was made, not in time, but simultaneously with time,' since it was only with the world's creation that change and motion, the measures of time, came into existence.[5] By contrast, Milton argues that motion and time could have existed before the world was made, noting that although Aristotle linked these ideas to our world he 'nevertheless pronounces the world itself to be eternal.'[6] In the same vein Raphael, the historian of celestial events in *Paradise Lost*, affirms that time, the measure of motion, provides for the categories of past, present, and future in eternity even as on earth (v, 577–84):

> As yet this world was not ...
>   when on a day
> (For time, though in Eternitie, appli'd
> To motion, measures all things durable
> By present, past, and future) on such day
> As Heav'n's great Year brings forth.

Behind this difference is a more striking departure from the Christian commonplace that in God's eternity before the world was made there is 'no change at all.'[7] Milton's *Paradise Lost* and also his *Christian Doctrine* show this

4 Patrides, 'The Renaissance View of Time: A Bibliographical Note,' *N & Q*, x (November 1963), 408–10
5 Augustine, *The City of God* XI, 6, *Basic Writings of Saint Augustine*, ed. Whitney J. Oates, 2 vols. (New York 1948), II, 148
6 *Works* xv, 35; cf. xv, 240
7 See Augustine, *City of God* XI, 6, *Basic Writings* II, 148

period to be rife with event and activity, causing change and development: the production of Chaos from the substance of God; the creation and revolt of the Angels; and even the generation of the Son who according to the *Christian Doctrine* was 'begotten of the Father in consequence of his decree, and therefore within the limits of time.'[8] This might mean simply that Milton in most unorthodox fashion pushes back the beginnings of the process of creation, and therefore the production of motion and time, to some point before the generation of the Son. But the difference may be more basic still, in that Milton nowhere proposes the classic and almost universally accepted formulation of God's eternity as an eternal present, a *nunc stans* in which measures of time are irrelevant. Speaking to this point Augustine had declared, 'All thy years stand at once. ... Thy years are one day, and Thy day is not daily, but to-day.'[9] For Luther, 'there is no Dinumeration of tyme with God' for whom 'all thynges are lapped up as it were in one bundle.' For Walter Charleton, God's realm 'knows no distinction of tenses.'[10] For Donne, 'All God's works are intire, and done in him, at once, and perfect as soon as begun.'[11] By contrast, Milton in the *Christian Doctrine* defines God's attribute of eternity to mean simply that he was 'always existant' without beginning or end; there is no hint of the eternal present.[12] Moreover, the tract as well as the epics portray God's realm as comprehending distinctions of tenses: prescience, for example, is identified as an aspect of God's wisdom whereby he 'perfectly foreknew in his own mind from the beginning what would be the nature and event of every

8 *Works* xv, 189
9 Augustine, *Confessions* xi, 13, *Basic Writings* i, 191
10 Luther, *A Commentarie ... uppon the twoo Epistles Generall of ... Peter, and Jude,* trans. Thomas Newton (London 1581), fol. 158; Walter Charleton, *The Darkness of Atheism* (London 1652), 118, cited in Patrides, 'Renaissance View of Time,' 410
11 *The Sermons of John Donne,* ed. George R. Potter and Evelyn M. Simpson, 10 vols. (Berkeley 1953–62), iv, 76–7
12 *Works* xiv, 43–7

future occurrence when its appointed season should arrive.'[13]

Both the eschewing of metaphysical speculation about God's eternal present and the insistence upon God's fore-knowledge are consonant with Milton's particular version of the Doctrine of Accommodation, according to which we are obligated to speak of God in biblical terms, however anthropomorphic, because the ineffable God has desired to be known by us in this way.[14] The Old Testament descriptions of a God involved with and constantly direct-ing the historical activities of his people, together with the Pauline vocabulary of foreknowledge, predestination, and prophecy, dictate for Milton (as for Hobbes)[15] the presentation of God as preeminently the God of History, acting within the temporal process. After the Second Coming process as such may be ended and time may (as Adam supposed) 'stand fixt' in a condition of full per-fection and consummation – though Milton never attempts in theology or poetry to describe such a condition of stasis. In any event it is clear that prior to the eschatological event God's eternity does not stand apart from time.

Besides manifesting his involvement with time and providing a perspective upon it, God's single speech in *Paradise Regained* also establishes categories for the interpretation of history, by authoritatively defining caus-ality and pattern in relation to the temptation episode. God's providential decree is identified as the primary cause of all events, with no causal role whatsoever reserved for Fate, Fortune, or Change: God's unequivocal statement in *Paradise Lost* is still true, 'Necessitie and Chance/ Approach not mee, and what I will is Fate' (VII, 172–3). The other important cause is the volition of intelligent

13 *Ibid.*, 75
14 *Ibid.*, 31–9
15 J.G.A. Pocock, 'Time, History and Eschatology in the Thought of Thomas Hobbes,' in *The Diversity of History: Essays in Honour of Herbert Butterfield*, ed. J.H. Elliott and H.G. Koenigsberger (New York 1970), 191–8

agents. The *Christian Doctrine* makes clear that God's foreknowledge is the basis of his providential decrees laid down from all eternity, but that neither his foreknowledge nor those providential decrees make for predestination or determinism, since among God's decrees is one reserving freedom of choice to all intelligent beings: 'he has decreed nothing absolutely which could happen otherwise through the liberty assigned to man.'[16] Accordingly, though the Father has foreseen the outcome of the temptation episode, the event is actually determined by the choices made and actions taken by the glorious Eremite, who has now emptied himself of all consciousness and awareness of his former condition in heaven.[17] The angelic chorus therefore rightly emphasizes the Father's confidence in the Son's virtue as the basis of his 'security' in venturing the trial (I, 176–9):

> The Father knows the Son; therefore secure
> Ventures his filial Vertue, though untri'd,
> Against whate're may tempt, whate're seduce,
> Allure, or terrifie, or undermine.

In addition, the Father's speech concerns itself with historical pattern defined in terms of typology. He highlights events in the past which have foreshadowed the temptation episode and other aspects of Christ's life and mission, and he intimates that the antitypical events about to take place will recapitulate these types. But according to God's providential plan the challenge laid upon Christ is not only to recapitulate the types but also to surpass and fulfill them: about to be tempted like Adam and Job, Christ must show himself an abler Job, a victorious Adam. Satan, declares the Father (I, 146–55),

16 *Works*, XIV, 77
17 See Lewalski, *Milton's Brief Epic*, chapter 6, for argument and documentation in support of this view.

>   might have learnt
> Less over-weening, since he fail'd in *Job*,
> Whose constant perseverance overcame
> Whate're his cruel malice could invent.
> He now shall know I can produce a man
> Of female Seed, far abler to resist
> All his sollicitations, and at length
> All his vast force, and drive him back to Hell,
> Winning by Conquest what the first man lost
> By fallacy surpriz'd.

Moreover, the shifts in time and tense in the Father's speech also mark the temptation episode as an epitome of Christ's forthcoming life and mission, and of the history of his church. He is here to lay down the 'rudiments' or first principles of that entire ongoing struggle with Sin and Death, and the tense shifts imperceptibly merge this action with all the future (I, 155–67):

>   But first I mean
> To exercise him in the Wilderness;
> There he shall first lay down the rudiments
> Of his great warfare, e're I send him forth
> To conquer Sin and Death the two grand foes,
> By Humiliation and strong Sufferance:
> His weakness shall o'recome Satanic strength
> And all the world, and mass of sinful flesh;
> That all the Angels and Ætherial Powers,
> They now, and men hereafter may discern,
> From what consummate vertue I have chose
> This perfect Man, by merit call'd my Son,
> To earn Salvation for the Sons of men.

According to the Father's sense of historical pattern, the temptation episode about to occur is the turning point of history, a reprise of the past which at the same time may fulfill and subsume its types in the discovery of a more excellent way, a genuine new departure which contains all the hope of the future.

Satan's sense of time and Satan's philosophy of history are the fruit of weary centuries of experience with the ways of the world, and these considerations dictate much of his strategy and behaviour during the temptation episode. In regard to causality in history, Satan had reason to know that the curse pronounced upon himself and the ordinances concerning the Messiah are decrees of God's Providence; but despite this his speeches suggest that Fate is the source of such ordinances and the ultimate cause of historical events. Similarly, though his own case shows and his temptation strategy presupposes that the free choice of men and angels is also an important historical cause, his speeches associate with this cause the arbitrary power of Fortune or Chance.[18] He is of the party of erring Roman historians whom Augustine denounced for attributing the greatness of Rome to these two causes, calling 'those things *fortuitous* which either have no causes, or such causes as do not proceed from some intelligible order, and those things *fatal* which happen independently of the will of God and man, by the necessity of a certain *order*.'[19] And he belongs among the vain philosophers whom Christ condemns in this poem for their ignorance of Divine Providence and their accusation of God 'under usual names,/ Fortune and Fate, as one regardless quite/ Of mortal things' (IV, 316–18).

Satan's language is, in part, a rhetorical strategy forwarding the temptation by insinuating a false view of God's providential design, but it derives also from the intellectual blindness which, according to Milton's theo-

18 Interestingly enough, Sir Walter Raleigh begins his *History of the World* (London 1614) by discussing problems of historical cause in just these terms, identifying God's Providence as the primary cause of all things, Nature as a secondary cause, and Fate and Fortune as having no causal agency whatsoever.

19 *City of God* v, 1, in *Basic Writings* II, 54

logical and poetic vision, affects all those who commit themselves to evil. In *Paradise Lost*, we recall that the fallen angels (like classical philosophers) were unable to resolve metaphysical questions of causality, and 'reason'd high/ Of Providence, Foreknowledge, Will, and Fate,/ Fixt Fate, free will, foreknowledge absolute,/ And found no end, in wandring mazes lost' (II, 558–61). In *Paradise Regained*, by referring to God's decrees in the passive voice and by means of intransitive verbs, by describing them as emanating from a generalized, impersonal 'heaven,' by punning constantly on the adjective 'fatal,' by undertaking to read Christ's fate in the stars, Satan insinuates that Fate, not God, is the source of such decrees. Alternatively, Satan ascribes events to Chance or Fortune. Approaching Christ, who has been led onto the desert by the Spirit, Satan inquires, 'Sir, what ill chance hath brought thee to this place' (I, 321). Soon after, recognized and challenged by Christ, he presents himself as one cast down by Fortune's wheel: ' 'Tis true, I am that Spirit unfortunate,/ Who leagu'd with millions more in rash revolt/ Kept not my happy Station' (I, 358–60). Satan apparently believes, or affects to believe, that some few matters such as the curse upon himself in the woman's seed and the decree for the establishment of Christ's kingdom are fated to occur, but that all else, including the means and the times for working out these fated events, is in the domain of Fortune.[20]

This is essentially a Roman perspective, prominent in those historians and poets who celebrated the interaction of Fate and Fortune in the founding and glorious development of the empire, and thus it is very appropriate to Satan in his self-chosen role of political advisor to Christ in the establishment of his own kingdom. In the classical

20 Dennis H. Burden, *The Logical Epic*, (Cambridge, Mass. 1967), 57–75 shows that Satan's thesis, or case, in that poem is also grounded upon ideas of fate or chance.

world Fate, sometimes personified as the *Parcae*, signified either irrevocable destiny controlling even the gods, or else natural necessity determined by the conjunction of the stars. The other cause beyond human control, Fortune, was taken to be an irrational, incalculable force haphazardly dispensing opportunities, benefits, or reverses; it was personified as the Goddess Fortuna, a fickle mistress who might reward the unworthy but who was often attracted by or mastered by human virtue, will, and daring – as the commonplace *'audaces, fortuna juvat'* indicates.[21] Livy, unfolding the history of Rome from its foundation to the Augustan age, manifested the characteristic Roman tendency to appeal to both forces but to emphasize the role of Fortune: he explained the birth of the city as fated and often referred to Scipio Aficanus as *'fatalis dux,'* but alluded much more frequently to the constant activity of Fortune in shaping events.[22] Moreover, like many Roman writers, Livy often tended to blur the conceptual differences between these two supernatural forces, as his formulation of Hannibal's surrender speech to Scipio indicates:

> If it was foreordained by fate that I, who ... have so often had the victory almost in my grasp, should come forward to sue for peace, I rejoice that destiny has given me you, and no one else, to whom I should bring my suit. ... This also may prove to have been Fortune's mocking sport, that having taken up arms when your Father was consul, and having fought with him my first battle with a Roman general, I come to his son unarmed to sue for peace.[23]

21 For a summary of various positions see Cicero, 'De Fato,' in *De Oratore*, et al., trans. H. Rackham, Loeb Library (London 1942); 'De Divinatione,' trans. W.A. Falconer, Loeb Library (London 1923).
22 Livy, *The History of Rome* I, 4, xxx, 28, trans. B.O. Foster et al., 13 vols. Loeb Library (London 1922–59), I, 11; VIII, 469
23 *Ibid.*, xxx, 1, *History of Rome*, Loeb, VIII, 473

This disposition is even more strikingly evidenced in the *Aeneid* when King Evander explains his arrival in Latium through the agency of these two interacting (though hardly distinguishable) forces: 'Myself, from fatherland an outcast, and seeking the ends of the sea, almighty Fortune and inevitable Fate planted on this soil.'[24]

As Roman historian and political theorist, Satan also gives primary emphasis to the role of Fortune in history, though unlike some of the Roman writers he distinguishes that agency sharply from Fate. Beginning with the realm of Fortuna he first urges upon Christ the desirability of foreseeing, and then of attempting to master, the turns of Fortune, insinuating the usefulness to this purpose of oracles and portents. These were often supposed to concern the domain of Fate (as in the case of Oedipus), but in *De Divinatione* the defender of oracles, dreams, and various kinds of portents associates divination with the province of Fortune – 'the foreseeing and foretelling of events considered as happening by chance.'[25] He explains further that oracles and portents are sent from the gods to aid men to 'foretell what will occur unless precautions are taken.'[26] This is Satan's posture in relation to Christ: substituting himself for the pagan gods as the giver of oracles and portents, and even blasphemously rewriting history by claiming to be the Father's oracle on occasion, Satan intimates his willingness to aid Christ by these means to understand the chances and changes awaiting him in the future, so that he may better direct his life.

Throughout the Kingdoms' temptation Satan continues to belabour Christ with advice as to the best way to make use of Fortune – now understood as the special opportunities or disadvantages which Christ will encounter in his

24 *Aeneid*, VIII, 332–6, *Virgil*, trans. H. Rushton Fairclough, Loeb Library (London 1960), II, 83
25 Cicero, 'De Divinatione' I, v, Loeb, 223
26 *Ibid.*, I, xvi, Loeb, 259

destined rise to Kingship. Satan's advice evidently derives
from – or rather, in the terms of the poem, is seen to
prefigure – Machiavelli's recommendations in *The Prince*.
To begin with, that work supplies the rationale for
Satan's contrivance of the visions of Parthia and Rome
as a means to provide Christ with vicarious experience of
statecraft. Machiavelli affirms that 'it is not likely that one
who has always lived as a private citizen, unless he be of
rare wit and character, will know how to command,'[27] and
Satan engages through the visions to remedy just such a
lack in Christ (III, 240–9):

> The wisest, unexperienc't, will be ever
> Timorous and loath ...
> Irresolute, unhardy, unadventrous:
> But I will bring thee where thou soon shalt quit
> Those rudiments, and see before thine eyes
> The Monarchies of the Earth, thir pomp and state,
> Sufficient introduction to inform
> Thee, of thy self so apt, in regal Arts,
> And regal Mysteries.

Machiavelli observes that, as a general rule, 'becoming a
prince from private station presupposes either character
or fortune,'[28] and his analysis of the predicament of the
ruler who seeks to rise by fortune explains the thrust of
Satan's comments in the wealth temptation – as well as
what he judiciously omits to say:

> They who rise from a private station to rulership merely
> by fortune have few difficulties in their ascent, but
> many in retaining their position. The path upward is easy
> for they fly. ... In this class we may place those who are
> awarded a state either for money or as a favor from

27 Niccolo Machiavelli, *The Prince*, trans. T.G. Bergin (New York
  1947), 17
28 *Ibid.*, 14

the giver. ... Of like sort were those emperors who came
to the purple from the condition of simple citizens
through the corruption of the soldiery. Princes of this
stamp depend absolutely on the will or fortune of those
who have raised them up, and both are unreliable and
insecure foundations. ... Either you are already a prince
or you are on the way to becoming one, and in the first
case generosity is harmful while in the second it is very
necessary to be considered open-handed.[29]

Satan builds upon all these precepts. He points out that
Christ's rise to high position from private station will be
extremely difficult – 'Thou art unknown, unfriended, low
of birth,/ A Carpenter thy Father known, thy self/ Bred
up in poverty' (II, 413–15). Satan offers therefore to play
kingmaker, supplying the wealth Christ will need to
corrupt and to support followers and soldiers. And by a
telling *double entendre* also found in Machiavelli, Satan's
claim to wealth extends to a claim of proprietorship over
the whole domain of Fortuna: 'Riches are mine, Fortune
is in my hands' (II, 429).

But Christ understands Machiavellian principles better
than Satan does, and he has Machiavelli's support as well as
that of more reputable moralists in his rejoinder that
kingdoms are safer if founded on character (virtue) than
on fortune.[30] Then Satan promptly makes this position
his own, but incorporates into his formulation of it
Miachiavelli's dictum that even princes of the highest
ability and virtue are dependent upon Fortune for opportunities and occasions, and ought to have force at their
command:

To come to those who through their own ability and not
through fortune have become princes, I shall cite as the
most excellent Moses, Cyrus, Romulus, Theseus, and
the like. ... And examining their lives and deeds we shall

29 *Ibid.*, 16–17, 46   30 *Ibid.*, 14

see that they got nothing from fortune save the occasions which gave them the opportunity of introducing the forms of government which they thought best. Without opportunity their valor and wisdom would have been of no avail, and without their talents the opportunity would have been missed. ... Cyrus had to find the Persians discontented with the rule of the Medes and the latter weak and effeminate from a long period of peace. Nor could Theseus have exhibited his talents if he had not found the Athenians dispersed. Such opportunities were lucky for these men, and their own native abilities seized the occasion whence their countries were ennobled and made happy. ... It is further necessary to inquire whether such innovators ... must ask help of others to carry on their work or can use force. In the first case they almost always come to a bad end and accomplish nothing but when they ... are able to use force they rarely fail. Hence all armed prophets have been successful, and all unarmed have come to ruin.[31]

In this vein Satan insists that both Christ's 'godlike virtues' and the destiny which has 'ordain'd' him King of Israel require him to seize the occasion offered by Fortune to take up arms for the purpose of regaining his kingdom (III, 163–73):

> Think'st thou to regain
> Thy right by sitting still or thus retiring?
> So did not *Machabeus:* he indeed
> Retir'd unto the Desert, but with arms;
>
> ...
>
> If Kingdom move thee not, let move thee Zeal,
> And Duty; Zeal and Duty are not slow;
> But on Occasions forelock watchful wait.

31 *Ibid.*, 14–15. Cf. Francesco Guicciardini, *Ricordi.* Series C 30, 31, *Maxims & Reflections of a Renaissance Statesman*, trans. Mario Domandi (New York 1965), 49

The passage derives further significance from the iconographical tradition, noted by Panofsky, which conflates the figure of the winged Goddess Fortuna with that of the bald-headed Occasion with her long forelock.[32] The availability of the Parthian military forces (which Christ is just in time to view) is presented by Satan as yet another fortunate opportunity afforded to Christ to establish his kingdom, and still more important, to maintain it against the power of Rome. Moreover, the degenerate condition of the Roman Empire in Christ's day offers a fortunate opportunity of another kind, similar to that which benefited Cyrus: the depraved, hated, and childless Tiberius would be an easy target for a *coup d'état* provoked by Christ's regal virtues, and in this way Christ could take over the entire Empire.

In the storm sequence Satan abandons the effort to direct Christ's actions through Fortune and turns to Fate, asserting that he can 'foretell' Christ's fate by reading the stars. This association of the stars with Fate was, as Augustine pointed out, a commonplace:

> When men hear that word [Fate], according to the ordinary use of the language, they simply understand by it the virtue of that particular position of the stars which may exist at the time when any one is born or conceived, which some separate altogether from the will of God, whilst others affirm that this also is dependent on that will.[33]

Satan's prognostication is that, since Christ has refused to take advantage of Fortune – the aid offered him by Satan 'which would have set thee in short time with ease/ On *David's* Throne; or Throne of all the world' (IV, 378–9), and since he has let pass the opportune time for action, 'full age, fulness of time, thy season,/ When Prophecies of thee

32 Erwin Panofsky, *Studies in Iconology* (New York 1967), 71–3; see Andrea Alciati, *Emblemata*, Emblem CXXI, 'Occasio.'
33 Augustine, *City of God* V, 1, *Basic Writings* II, 55

are best fulfill'd' (IV, 380–1), he must now abide the harsh
Fate spelled out for him in the stars (IV, 382–93):

> If I read aught in Heaven,
> Or Heav'n write aught of Fate, by what the Stars
> Voluminous, or single characters,
> In their conjunction met, give me to spell,
> Sorrows, and labours, opposition, hate,
> Attends thee, scorns, reproaches, injuries,
> Violence and stripes, and lastly cruel death,
> A Kingdom they portend thee, but what Kingdom,
> Real or Allegoric I discern not,
> Nor when, eternal sure, as without end,
> Without beginning; for no date prefixt
> Directs me in the Starry Rubric set.

Satan's claim for the power of the stars constitutes a modest
variety of what the Renaissance termed Judicial Astrology:
modest, because he does not claim that the stars of themselves determine events or control man's fate. However,
his assumption of the certainty of the stars' predictions, and
his attendant disposition to regard Fate rather than the
Providence of God as the source of the predictions, is
enough to make him liable to the usual theological cen-
sures.[34] Calvin, a moderate on the astrology issue, found
some validity in Natural Astrology – the science of the ways
in which heavenly bodies influence material bodies, including our own. He granted also that God might sometimes use the stars as secondary causes, 'as a preparation to
accomplyshe hys worke even so as he determined in his
eternall counsell,'[35] but he categorically denied the relia-
bility of astrological predictions on the ground that man's
lot is determined by God's will, not the natural course of

34 See Don C. Allen, *The Star-Crossed Renaissance* (Durham, NC
    1941)
35 John Calvin, *An Admonicion against Astrology Judiciall and other
    curiosities* ... trans. G.G. [ylby] (London 1561), Sigs Bi, Cii

stellar conjunctions. He concluded that those who credit the stars with 'foretelling that which shall fal upon them all their life longe, and the time and maner of their deathe ... [show] nothing but a rashe boldnes and no reason at all.'[36] Since Satan's horoscope for Christ is within its limits true – i.e., Christ will indeed suffer and die in the way Satan indicates – we must assume either that God is here using the stars to announce and further his designs, or else, more probably, that Satan disingenuously affects to read in the stars information which he already had, as Christ did, from the Old Testament prophets. In addition, though Satan's scornful allusions to the ambiguities surrounding the beginning of Christ's kingdom serve his rhetorical purposes, they also display his literal-mindedness, his myopic inability to penetrate the true meaning of the signs he affects to be reading. For of course God's decree provides, paradoxically, that the suffering which is Christ's 'fate' is precisely the means to his Kingdom: the means as well as the ends are part of God's providential order.

Satan next contrives violent tempests, ugly dreams, and lightnings to confirm his interpretation of Christ's fate, and then, disclaiming all responsibility for them, he intimates that these portents and prodigies testify Heaven's displeasure over Christ's failure to act. He here moves beyond Judicial Astrology and Fate to an implied recognition of God's providence as he invokes the well-nigh universal Renaissance belief that disorders and prodigies are signs of God's wrath for our sins.[37] Calvin's formulation is again typical:

> Neither famines, pestilences, nor warres, come at any tyme by the disposition of the starres: if it be not because god would declare his wrath upon mankinde. ... Sinnes

36 *Ibid.*, Sig B v
37 See C.A. Patrides, *Milton and the Christian Tradition* (Oxford 1966), 71–9. Dick Taylor, 'The Storm Scene in *Paradise Regained*,' *UTQ* xxiv (1955), 359–76, has discussed some of these implications.

are the woode to kyndle God's wrathe, for the which
wars, famine, pestilence, hayle, frost and other lyke
thynges do come. ... When God wyll stretche out his
hande to execute some judgement worthy to be remem-
bred in the worlde, he wyll some tymes admonishe us by
comets.[38]

Satan intimates that Christ is the object of these portents
because his passivity denotes his submission to Fate as
ruling force, and thereby proves him unfaithful to the mission God his given him (IV, 465–83):

This Tempest at this Desert most was bent;
Of men at thee, for only thou here dwell'st.
Did I not tell thee, if thou didst reject
The perfect season offer'd with my aid
To win thy destin'd seat, but wilt prolong
All to the push of Fate, persue thy way
Of gaining *David's* Throne no man knows when,
For both the when and how is no where told ...
           be sure to find,
What I foretold thee, many a hard assay
Of dangers, and adversities and pains,
Ere thou of *Israel's* Scepter get fast hold;
Whereof this ominous night that clos'd thee round,
So many terrors, voices, prodigies
May warn thee, as a sure fore-going sign.

But as Christ acidly points out, Satan's theory of prodigies
as testimonials of God's displeasure is quite beside the
point since these prodigies were contrived by Satan – 'not
sent from God, but thee' (IV, 491).

    Satan's sense of the cyclical movement of time and his
concomitant belief in recurrent and repetitive patterns in
history are also fundamental to his action in the temptation

38 Calvin, *Admonicion against Astrology Judiciall*, Sigs. c iv, D v,
    D vii

episode. In these matters also he resembles some classical historians.[39] Thucydides, appealing to the concept of unchanging human nature, believed that his work would prove useful to anyone who wished 'to have a clear view both of the events which have happened and of those which will some day, in all human probability, happen again in the same or a similar way,' the same situations necessarily producing the same responses.[40] Polybius, the Greek historian who came to Rome in the second century BC, identified as a 'cause appointed by nature' the development and decline of states according to a cyclical pattern; accordingly, he thought the laws of history could predict accurately how 'constitutions change, disappear, and finally return to the point from which they started.'[41] Still more basic to Satan's sense of the dreary round of historical recurrence is the conception voiced by the Stoic Marcus Aurelius:

> Consider the past; such great changes of political supremacies. You may foresee also the things which will be. For they will certainly be of like form, and it is not possible that they should deviate from the order of things which takes place now. To have contemplated human life for forty years is the same as to have contemplated it for ten thousand years. For what more will you see?[42]

Satan's similar sense of eternal recurrence, of the 'circling hours' locking him into an inevitable doom, produces

39 See Roger L. Shinn, 'Augustinian and Cyclical Views of History,' *Anglican Theological Review* XXXI (1949), 133–41; Charles N. Cochrane, *Christianity and Classical Culture* (Oxford 1957), 399–516
40 Thucydides, *The History of the Peloponnesian War*, I, 22, III, 82–5, trans. Charles Foster Smith, Loeb Library (New York 1921), I, 41, II, 143–53
41 Polybius, *The Histories* VI, 9, trans. W.R. Paton, Loeb Library (New York 1923), III, 289
42 Marcus Aurelius, *Meditations* VII, 49, trans. George Long, *Essential Works of Stoicism*, ed. Moses Hadas (New York 1961), 157

in him two styles of behaviour, two attitudes toward time. On the one hand he displays a precipitate opportunism which attempts to break out of habitual patterns but cannot do so. In his consult in mid-air Satan forestalls long debate such as is portrayed in *Paradise Lost* by insisting that 'something sudden' be undertaken immediately to prevent the approaching doom. Later, proposing himself as a model for Christ, Satan dissembles his true motivations but justifies his predilection for hasty action (III, 209–24):

> I would be at the worst; worst is my Port,
> My harbour and my ultimate repose,
> The end I would attain, my final good.
>
> ...
>
> If I then to the worst that can be hast,
> Why move thy feet so slow to what is best.

Another of Satan's challenges to Christ also affords a momentary glimpse of the cynicism and opportunism he usually hides more effectively: 'Raign then; what canst thou better do the while?' (III, 180). On the other hand, Satan's behaviour displays a sterile repetitiveness as, defeated by Christ, he returns again and again only to be repulsed as many times. This style of action mimics the repetitiveness of nature and history as Satan conceives of it, and the narrator emphasizes the point by a series of expressive similies (IV, 15–24):

> ...As a swarm of flies in vintage time,
> About the wine-press where sweet moust is powr'd,
> Beat off, returns as oft with humming sound;
> Or surging waves against a solid rock,
> Though all to shivers dash't, the assault renew,
> Vain batt'ry, and in froth or bubbles end;
> So Satan, whom repulse upon repulse
> Met ever, and to shameful silence brought,
> Yet gives not o're though desperate of success,
> And his vain importunity pursues.

As the term 'importunity' suggests, these two styles of action come at last to the same thing; Satan is driven, compulsive, utterly unable to respond creatively to time. He is unable to say with the best of the pagans, 'Ripeness is all,' or with Mary and the Apostles and Christ to expect providential fulfillment, re-creation, in the fulness of time.

This conception of historical pattern as eternal recurrence and this compulsive attitude toward time lead Satan to base his temptations of Christ upon the premise that Christ's behaviour must inevitably repeat the patterns set by men before him. The assumption is part of his temptation strategy, but it is also part of the self-inflicted blindness which attends his rejection of providential history: he can conceive of no new thing under the sun. At the outset he designs his own role and bases his hope for success upon the imitation of past precedent (I, 100–5):

> I, when no other durst, sole undertook
> The dismal expedition to find out
> And ruine *Adam*, and the exploit perform'd
> Successfully; a calmer voyage now
> Will waft me; and the way found prosperous once
> Induces best to hope of like success.

His followers make the same assumption: they commit the task to Satan again as they did before, because his 'attempt/ At first against mankind so well had thriv'd' (I, 113–14). By the time of the second consult, however, Satan knows that he is facing something very different: he warns his followers that there is now 'Far other labour to be undergon/ Then when I dealt with *Adam* first of Men' (II, 132–3), and he encourages their realistic acceptance of the possibility of failure as well as their assistance in meeting the new challenge. Belial, however, evidences how very limited is the perspective of the fallen angels when he responds to this challenge by proposing that Satan again employ the method which caused Adam's fall, and that of wisest Solomon: 'Set women in his eye.' Satan, angered, accuses Belial of weighing all men by himself, whereas this youth is 'wiser far/ Then *Solomon*' (II, 205–6). But, ironically, Satan himself can only suggest lures used before to wreck others, things which have 'shew/ Of worth, of honour, glory, and popular praise;/ Rocks whereon greatest men have oftest wreck'd' (II, 226–8). And still more ironically, Satan can find nothing better for his next sequence of temptations (the banquet, wealth, and glory passages) than to repeat in them the essence of the temptations offered to Adam and Eve – sensuality, avarice, and vainglory, according to the widely-recognized Triple Equation formula.[43]

Satan's temptations to Christ assert again and again in one form or another the same motif: what happened before must happen again. He invites Christ to find in the examples of old, whether Hebrew or classical, whether recognized types of his mission or clear antitheses to him, literal and exact models for imitation. At his first approach to Christ he appeals at once to precedent: 'single none/ Durst ever, who return'd and dropt not here/ His Carcass, pin'd with hunger and with drougth' (I, 323–5). In the banquet temptation also he alludes to the 'Others of some note' – Hagar with Ishmael, the Israelites, Elijah – who were fed by God in this same desert, concluding that Christ should consider himself abandoned by God since 'Of thee these forty days none hath regard' (II, 315). Satan then undertakes himself to supply the food called for in the paradigm established by the types, though in more lavish style than God's provision of manna or pulse. The Satanic banquet has the appearance of being a new gesture, a breaking out of past moulds: 'How simple, to these Cates compar'd,/ Was that crude Apple that diverted *Eve*' (II, 348–9). But, ironically, the banquet is only a more lavish manipulation of that lure of sensuality which helped provoke Eve's desire

43 See Elizabeth Pope, *Paradise Regained : The Tradition and the Poem* (Baltimore 1947)

for the apple, and a more complicated version of forbidden fruit – for some of the foods Satan proffers are forbidden by Mosaic law and all of them fall under the immutable prohibition Paul enunciates against idolatrous eating at the Devil's table.[44]

In the wealth temptation Satan grounds his realpolitik upon the assumption of unchanging human nature – 'Money brings Honour, Friends, Conquest, and Realms' (II, 422) – and proposes as a model the vicious Antipater. In the glory temptation, more complexly, Satan's precipitate attitude toward time fuses with his belief in inevitable recurrence, as he undertakes to produce in Christ a compulsive youth-worship like that manifested by many famous conquerors of the world (III, 31–42):

> Thy years are ripe and over-ripe, the Son
> Of *Macedonian Philip* had e're these
> Won *Asia* and the Throne of *Cyrus* held
> At his dispose, young *Scipio* had brought down
> The *Carthaginian* pride, young *Pompey* quell'd
> The *Pontic* King and in triumph had rode.
> ...
> Great *Julius*, whom now all the world admires,
> The more he grew in years, the more inflam'd
> With glory, wept that he had liv'd so long
> Inglorious; but thou yet art not too late.

In the exchange over Zeal and Duty Satan argues that the same conditions which provoked Judas Maccabaeus to take up arms again obtain, and so should provoke the same response in Christ. In the exchange over Parthia, Satan insists that the only way for Christ to win and secure his kingdom of Israel is by battling its enemies, as David did. In the learning temptation Satan makes Christ's childhood

44 See Michael Fixler, 'The Unclean Meats of the Mosaic Law and the Banquet Scene in *Paradise Regained*,' MLN LXX (1955), 573–7; Lewalski, *Milton's Brief Epic*, 215–18

propensity to learned disputation with the rabbis an absolute mandate for the future – 'the childhood shews the man,/ As morning shews the day' (IV, 220–1). But in the course of this episode Satan appears to shift ground, assuming for the first time a respect for mature seasoning rather than youthful opportunism as he urges Christ to study the precepts afforded by the classical philosophers and orators, notably Socrates: 'These here revolve, or, as thou lik'st, at home,/ Till time mature thee to a Kingdom's waight' (IV, 281–8). Yet Satan has not really changed: according to his formulation, maturity and readiness will result automatically from time spent studying the learning of the past, and, as Christ points out, he has absolutely nothing to say about gaining the wisdom needed to evaluate books properly or to think creatively in new ways.

Just before the moment of truth on the Tower, Satan reveals that he still cannot get beyond the categories established by the past. In regard to his own case, he rings changes upon the ambiguities attendant upon the term, Son of God: 'The Son of God I also am, or was,/ And if I was, I am; relation stands;/ All men are Sons of God' (IV, 518–20). But relation, in Satan's simple meaning, does not stand; it can be radically altered as natures alter, and Satan is not now what once he was. Christ on the other hand still is the same Son of God that he was in heaven, the True Image of the Father, although neither he nor Satan know as yet the full meaning of the term 'Son' as applied to Christ. In this sequence Satan demonstrates that he has not begun to deal with the evidence before him, for he will not admit that he has seen anything here which he had not seen before. He has found Christ firm, 'To the utmost of meer man both wise and good,/ Not more; for Honours, Riches, Kingdoms, Glory/ Have been before contemn'd, and may agen' (IV, 535–7). What Satan cannot see, given his fixed categories, is that Christ has not only repeated these good models and types, but has subsumed and fulfilled them, and through this action has made novelty and re-creation possible – new men, new lives, in a new kingdom whose history need not be sterile repitition but can be marked by significant and unique events.[45]

The incarnate Christ is also profoundly concerned throughout *Paradise Regained* with perceptions of time and with questions of historical cause and pattern. Having emptied himself of that share in the Father's omniscience which was granted him in heaven, and lacking Satan's experience of having lived through and observed the whole course of history, Christ approaches the past as we do, through the written records – the Bible especially and also the classical sources. He understands from the outset, though, that the ultimate cause of the historical process is Divine Providence, not Fate or Fortune, and that the free choices of intelligent beings are also causes. Christ has studied history primarily for its didactic and prophetic dimension, seeking through it to define his own role and mission. His opening soliloquy indicates that he has pored over the scripture records in order to 'learn and know, and thence to do/ What might be publick good' (I, 203–4), and that he has considered various roles suggested by his reading, including the office of military deliverer. Negative historical examples have been instructive for him also: he knows the stories of Satan's deceits and practices against Job and others, knows the accounts of deceitful oracles misleading men, and knows of the proud and vicious would-be conquerors whose wars have laid waste the earth. In his encounters with Satan he can distinguish sharply between such despicable personages and those others worthy of 'memorial' and imitation – the Hebrew Judges, David, and the Roman republican heroes for their virtuous exercise of rule, and especially Socrates and Job for their 'deeds of

45 See Oscar Cullman, *Christ and Time: The Primitive Christian Conception of Time and History*, trans. Floyd V. Filson (Philadelphia 1951)

peace, by wisdom eminent,/ By patience, temperance' (III, 91–2).

To help determine his role, Christ has also reflected deeply upon the prophetic dimension of the Scripture, upon the stories of his own past, and upon the remarkable signs which have attended his life to date. From his mother he had the story of his miraculous conception, of the angelic prophecy that he would sit on David's throne, of the angelic testimony at his birth designating him the Messiah, and of the 'Star new-grav'n in Heaven' (I, 253) which guided the Magi to his cradle at his nativity. These true signs and portents led him back to the writings of the prophets for clarification (I, 259–63):

> Strait I again revolv'd
> The Law and Prophets, searching what was writ
> Concerning the Messiah, to our Scribes
> Known partly, and soon found of whom they spake
> I am.

From the same scriptural source he learned, in general terms, that his role will involve 'many a hard assay even to the death' (I, 264) as the means of compassing man's redemption. He has reflected also upon the recent signs – the dove and the voice from Heaven at his Baptism. This study of history in its prophetic aspect has taught Christ that he is himself the referent of all the prophecies, the focal point of the historical process; and he goes forth into the desert awaiting further revelation as he meditates 'of things past and to come' (I, 300).

But despite this awareness of his responsibility for the future course of history, and despite his realization that the time is 'now full' for beginning his mission, Christ's behaviour is neither anxious nor compulsive. Because he knows that the times and the seasons are in God's hands, he can wait upon the fullness of time for the fulfillment of the prophecies, and for clarification of their true meaning. He can live with incomplete knowledge (as Eve could not); he can engage in the constant, hard, intellectual effort required to distinguish true from false prophecy, true from false portents, the worse from the better models of conduct; and he can remain open and responsive to the continuing guidance of the Spirit. It is in this frame of mind – the Spirit leading – that he moves out onto the desert (I, 290–3):

> And now by some strong motion I am led
> Into this Wilderness, to what intent
> I learn not yet, perhaps I need not know;
> For what concerns my knowledge God reveals.

This openness permits him to build upon, but yet not be bound by, historical precedents and types, or by a literal interpretation of prophecy.

This confidence and openness is not maintained effortlessly, for this hero like any man can be cast into doubts and distress by the unexpected. Confronted with the new experience of hunger during his seemingly endless fast, he voices but soon overcomes such doubts (II, 245–56):

> Where will this end? four times ten days I have pass'd
> Wandring this woody maze, and humane food
> Nor tasted, nor had appetite: that Fast
> To Vertue I impute not, or count part
> Of what I suffer here; if Nature need not,
> Or God support Nature without repast
> Though needing, what praise is it to endure?
> But now I feel I hunger, which declares
> Nature hath need of what she asks; yet God
> Can satisfie that need some other way,
> Though hunger still remain.

The experience of doubt and fear in the face of the unexpected is magnified many times over in Christ's followers, who can hardly bear the thought that the Messiah whom they thought 'certainly now come' seems to have been rapt away from them. But then they reaffirm their confidence in God and their willingness to wait upon his seasons: 'let us wait; thus far he hath perform'd,/ ... Let us be glad of this, and all our fears/ Lay on his Providence; he will not fail/ ... Soon we shall see our hope, our joy return' (II, 49–57).

Despite the apparent uncertainties of his position, Christ firmly resists Satan's suggestion that the prophecies of his reign would be best fulfilled precipitously. Instead, he affirms his willingness to wait upon the due time, and more than that, to embrace whatever process of preparation God may have designed as the best means to ready him for his kingdom (III, 182–97):

> All things are best fulfil'd in their due time,
> And time there is for all things, Truth hath said:
> If of my raign Prophetic Writ hath told,
> That it shall never end, so when begin
> The Father in his purpose hath decreed,
> He in whose hand all times and seasons roul.
> What if he hath decreed that I shall first
> Be try'd in humble state, and things adverse,
> ...
> Suffering, abstaining, quietly expecting
> Without distrust or doubt, that he may know
> What I can suffer, how obey? who best
> Can suffer, best can do; best reign, who first
> Well hath obey'd; just tryal e're I merit
> My exaltation without change or end.

Similarly, though Christ proclaims the folly of endeavouring to liberate the idolatrous lost tribes while they are slaves to their own vices, he is confident that at the appointed time God's providence can work their inward reformation (III, 433–40):

> Yet he at length, time to himself best known,
> Remembring *Abraham*, by some wond'rous call
> May bring them back repentant and sincere,

And at their passing cleave the *Assyrian* flood,
While to their native land with joy they hast,

...

To his due time and providence I leave them.

In regard to the historical sequence Christ discerns pattern but not mere repetitions. Types are recapitulated in antitypes, but also surpassed; prophecies are fulfilled, but according to a higher spiritual meaning which transcends the literal terms. At the outset of the temptation episode Christ does not yet see himself as the fulfillment of the types or understand the full spiritual meaning of the prophecies, but he comes to such knowledge as he responds to Satan's complex challenges. As he perceives the necessity of refusing to recapitulate literally even the good models, the recognized types of Messiah's role and office, he proceeds to fulfill these types and prophecies by exalting each term to a new plane of spiritual value. As Christ works out his philosophy of history, what *has been* is the appropriate starting point but not the fixed definition of what *will be*. The historical process is seen to be linear, not cyclical, and Christian typology is shown to involve progress, redefinition, and re-creation.

In response to Satan's insinuation of the danger of starvation on the desert, Christ cites those other prophets cared for by God in the same desert, Moses and Elijah; later, under stress of hunger, he dreams of sharing with Elijah or Daniel the miraculous food provided to them by angels. But he resists the conclusion that these typological events must precisely repeat themselves: 'God/ Can satisfie that need some other way,/ Though hunger still remain' (II, 253–5). Spiritual food, moreover, is more important than physical: 'Man lives not by Bread only, but each Word/ Proceeding from the mouth of God' (I, 349–50), and the hungry Christ hungers yet more 'to do my Fathers will' (II, 259). Accordingly, Christ's recapitulation of the desert experience of the Israelites, of Moses, and of Elijah becomes an antitypical event in which he repudiates false prophecy, transcends the Law and the Prophets, and defines for his church a new order of prophecy and teaching which will significantly alter man's spiritual life (I, 460–4):

> God hath now sent his living Oracle
> Into the World to teach his final will,
> And sends his Spirit of Truth henceforth to dwell
> In pious Hearts, an inward Oracle
> To all truth requisite for men to know.

In the long sequence concerning Christ's kingship – the inner kingship over the self and the ordained public kingship over Israel – Christ indicates that he will in some sense recapitulate the rise from poverty to dominion exemplified in Gideon, Jepthah, and the Roman republican worthies: 'I/ May also in this poverty as soon/ Accomplish what they did, perhaps and more' (II, 450–2). The final phrase indicates openness to the redefinitions which the temptation sequence produces even in regard to those noblest types, Job and Socrates. At the conclusion of the sequence Christ is proclaimed by the narrator, and proclaims himself, Israel's true King, but now in a wholly spiritual sense: he has repudiated literal reign over David's literal kingdom; he has refused to imitate David and other worldly kings in establishing and defending his realm by military might; and he has defined his unique kingdom as involving the liberation of the spirit of man from bondage to his own wickedness – the only true and lasting liberation. He lays claim to David's kingdom, and all the kingdoms of the world, on the basis of Daniel's prophecy, now understood to refer to his spiritual kingdom and to the irresistible though wholly spiritual power it will exercise (IV, 146–51):

> Know therefore when my season comes to sit
> On *David's* Throne, it shall be like a tree
> Spreading and over-shadowing all the Earth,

> Or as a stone that shall to pieces dash
> All Monarchies besides throughout the world,
> And of my Kingdom there shall be no end.

Even the kingdoms of learning are to be superseded and transvalued, insofar as they are comprised of literal books, particular philosophers, and literary masterpieces asserted by Satan to be necessary to Christ's development in personal and political wisdom. Rather, Christ proclaims the power of the human spirit to move beyond all these, in response to the Light from above which was itself the source of whatever is true in any of them: 'Think not but that I know these things, or think/ I know them not ... he who receives/ Light from above, from the fountain of light,/ No other doctrine needs' (IV, 286–90). He observes further that (IV, 322–30),

> who reads
> Incessantly, and to his reading brings not
> A spirit and judgment equal or superior,
> (And what he brings, what needs he elsewhere seek)
> Uncertain and unsettl'd still remains,
> Deep verst in books and shallow in himself,
> Crude or intoxicate, collecting toys,
> And trifles for choice matters, worth a spunge;
> As Children gathering pibles on the shore.

This redefinition of wisdom puts Christ and his church in possession of the Kingdoms of the Mind in a spiritual rather than a literal form, and in possession of a wisdom which goes beyond the Socratic admission of ignorance. The new definition is the Jobean and Augustinian one – *Pietas est Sapientia*, the fear of the Lord is the beginning of wisdom.[46]

The tower temptation is a moment of epiphany or *kairos* in which, after enduring the full power of Satan

46 See Lewalski, *Milton's Brief Epic*, chapter 11, 281–302

for the full time prefixed, Christ at once perceives and manifests his identity as Son of God, and by that manifestation conquers Satan. Setting Christ on the pinnacle of the temple where by human power he cannot stand, Satan proposes again the literal enactment of a prophecy – Cast thyself down and angels will rescue thee. Instead, by simply remaining in the place where Satan's violence has thrust him, Christ enacts a foreshadowing of his priestly office, which involves the passive submission to Satanic violence in the crucifixion – a passion which, paradoxically, is itself the action of conquering Satan, Sin, and Death. In this moment the identity question is resolved: Christ has merited and receives illumination and power from above to manifest his Sonship, and Satan can no longer escape the unbearable truth (iv, 561–2):

> Tempt not the Lord thy God, he said and stood.
> But Satan smitten with amazement fell.

After this, angels bear Christ from his uneasy station to a heavenly banquet and glorify him as the 'True Image of the Father' (iv, 596), one with the First-born who long ago 'debelled' Satan from heaven. His victory in the wilderness recapitulates that earlier victory but also surpasses it, in that this victory recreates and restores mankind: 'now thou hast aveng'd/ Supplanted *Adam*, and by vanquishing/ Temptation, hast regain'd lost Paradise' (iv, 606–8). The tense changes in the angel's song, like the analogous tense shifts in the Father's speech, project this event forward into the future: Christ has now founded the Paradise within but will only establish it 'when time shall be/ Of Tempter and Temptation without fear' (iv, 616–17). He has now conquered Satan, but that conquest only foreshadows Satan's forthcoming fall like an Autumnal Star or lightning at Christ's crucifixion, as well as his last and deadliest wound at the end of time. The Angelic hymn hereby confirms the

Father's earlier designation of the temptation episode as the epitome of human history; in it Christ has subsumed the past, and by working out the rudiments of his great warfare has released all the potentialities which the future may hold. History will now move forward to its final end, but from this climactic moment on a higher plane, for the Paradise within now restored to man means – among other things – new possibilities for uniqueness and creativity within the domain of Time and History.

'TO WHICH IS ADDED

SAMSON AGONISTES-'

BALACHANDRA RAJAN

An intensive examination of a crucial passage in *Paradise Lost* may seem a perverse way of beginning what is after all, a paper on *Paradise Regained* and *Samson Agonistes*. Nevertheless the adopting of the strategy of indirect approach (to use the term coined by a noted military historian) can serve to expound the intricacies and felicities of Milton's sense of design. By not taking the shortest route to the subject we can show what longer routes bring into the field of relevance and thereby suggest something of the nature of that field. It is not likely that the wanderings of this essay will have the profound pertinence of the digressions in *Lycidas*; but in so far as the wanderings remain answerable to the work, they should bear witness to the work's cohesive strategies and to the place which the final poems occupy in that cohesiveness. The interrelationships created between Milton's major poems call on each poem to comment on and to help in defining the

others. The search for the overall understanding can therefore begin and begin significantly wherever the attention
is sufficiently engrossed.

At an important turn in the movement of *Paradise Lost*
(the word 'crisis' is studiously refrained from), Adam and
Eve, having confessed their responsibility in identical
cadences against the gathering force of an anarchy which
they themselves have let loose, return to the place of their
judgement and prostrate themselves in 'prayer unfeigned
and humiliation meek.' This brief episode has one surprising feature: it is spread over two books of the poem.
Because of this device the small beginning can be magnified
and the event can be seen both as climax and as prelude –
answering the expansion of evil into space and counter-
poising its expansion into history.

If this were all, we would be looking at a deft enough
piece of carpentry but not one that, given the standard of
Milton's structural accomplishment, would merit more
than an editorial footnote. What is taking place is not
simply the distribution of a force along two lines of movement. We are also being helped by virtue of the placing to
ascertain something of the nature of the force. Two books
allow us two perspectives. There is first the existential
progress from recognition to the amending response and
then the cosmic perspective which enables us to esteem
the fruit of responsibility rightly exercised, as worth more
than the fruit of all the trees of Paradise. Looking forward
from Christ's words (XI, 22–30) we can see them as an
intimation of the coming reality of the paradise within.

The knowledge that we are considering an event along
two lines of vision helps us to confirm the basic rightness
of what is usually treated as an inconsistency. In X, 1099
Adam and Eve are described as 'prostrate.' In XI, 1 we are
told that they 'stood.' It is true that Milton tells us in the
De Doctrina (*Col.* XVII, 90) that 'no particular posture of
the body in prayer was enjoined' but whatever posture was

chosen ought to have been sustained for more than seven
lines. The passage to another book makes less obtrusive
what seems to be a lapse and there is no reason why we
should vex the lapse into an aesthetic irritant. But the
situation changes when we remember that standing in the
longer view, is the opposite of falling, that regeneration is
spoken of four lines later and that if 'stood' is read in
this sense, the interplay with 'lowliest plight' is energised,
providing us with much more than a local paradox.[1] Rising
through falling is one of the poem's fundamental ironies
and if we now move back to the 'humiliation meek' which
is the closing stance of the tenth book, we cannot but
contrast it both in its spirit and in its consequences, with
the humiliation of pride which Satan suffers on his return
to hell. The two events are in the same book and the
contrast is one of tone as well as of significance – Pande-
monium's suddenly monstrous lavishness and the simplicity of the temple of the upright heart. Finally, because
the word humiliation is so sparingly used by Milton (on
only one other occasion in *Paradise Lost*, according to
Bradshaw), we may be able to remember III, 313–14, with
its basic distinction between reality and appearance

> Therefore thy Humiliation shall exalt
> With thee thy Manhood also to this Throne

In reading a crucial passage by Milton, we often find it
extending back into the whole poem, bringing progressively
wider out-reachings of relevance into the immediacy of its
life. The rhetorical repetition at the end of the tenth book,

---

1   It is possible to reconcile 'prostrate' with 'stood' on the lines
    suggested by Pearce and Greenwood (*The Poetical Works of John
    Milton*, ed. Henry J. Todd, London 1842, note on XI, 1) and later
    by Carey and Fowler (*The Poems of John Milton*, London 1968,
    note on XI, 1). But the acceptance of the paradox as deliberate (a
    possibility which Carey and Fowler later suggest) results in a far
    more satisfying reading.

curiously stilted to the modern reader, can be defended
as emphasizing the solemnity of the decision[2] and also as
indicating that even the infected will (as Sidney terms it)
can respond fully to the movement towards righteousness.
Intention and execution are one and the act holds nothing
back from the undertaking. But both the repetition and the
context strongly recall a similar device in the third book
(III, 188–93):[3]

> I will cleer thir senses dark,
> What may suffice, and soft'n stonie hearts
> To pray, repent, and bring obedience due.
> To Prayer, repentance, and obedience due,
> Though but endevord with sincere intent,
> Mine ear shall not be slow, mine eye not shut.

Hughes's note on III, 190 makes the connection with
book x but it needs to be added that the last lines of this
book are concerned primarily with prayer. It is not until the
eleventh book that repentance is mentioned and Adam, by
not using the word, helps to preserve it in its theological
signification. When the term is employed the language of
regeneration falls into position around it – the upward
movement is thus seen to be latent in the humbling. The
division across two books expounds with subtle care the
nature of a spiritual process and also testifies to an undertaking made good. 'Obedience due' is to come considerably
later – in fact not until XII, 561 when Adam declares
'Henceforth I learne, that to obey is best.'

Other connections with Book III declare themselves.
'Mercy first and last shall brightest shine' (III, 134) is God's
preface to the dialogue that expounds the mystery of the
redemption and Adam in remembering the severity of his

2 *The Complete Poetical Works of John Milton*, ed. Douglas Bush
  (Boston 1965), note on x, 1098–1104
3 All quotations of the poetry are from the Columbia edition.

judge recalls the shining of mercy in his countenance
(x, 1096).[4] In x, 1061 Adam hopes that God will 'incline' to
pity and the phrase he uses is twice sung by the angels in
the solemn music after the celestial dialogue (iii, 402, 405).
The angels are contrasting man's fate with that of Satan
and in Book x we are seeing the contrast revived. Adam's
decision to pray at the place of judgement, a decision put
in his mind by Eve (x, 1086–7, 932–4) recognizes the
relationship between justice and mercy, but not necessarily
the content of that relationship. In the human perspective,
mercy is felt as forgiveness and a waiving of justice. But
cosmic justice cannot be waived if the principles of order
are to remain in the nature of things. The answer to what
the angels describe as the strife of justice and mercy (iii,
406–7) lies not in the suspension of the lower principle but
in superseding 'The rigid satisfaction, death for death'
(iii, 212) by the higher satisfaction of the atonement. Adam
cannot see this but we are encouraged to the larger understanding by the Miltonic innovation which makes Christ
Adam's judge as well as his redeemer,[5] by the descent of
mercy at the place of justice (xi, 2) and by the persistent
affiliations with Book iii which we now see as woven into
the repentance.

Disaffiliations from Hell are also called for. For Satan,
repentance is submission to the deified force of a conqueror.
It is 'to bow and sue for grace/ With suppliant knee.' (i,
111–12).[6] Adam and Eve can regain their dignity out of
their 'lowliest plight' because they have learned to humble
themselves more profoundly. Mammon's caustic dismissal
of 'warbl'd Hymns,' 'Forc't Halleluiahs,' and servile offer-

4 Carey and Fowler on x, 1096–7
5 D. Taylor Jr, 'Milton's Treatment of the Judgment and Expul-
   sion in *Paradise Lost*,' *Tulane Studies in English*, x (1960), 71
6 Satan sees the possibility of humbling himself as ignominious and
   shameful (i, 115–16). Christ (xii, 406, 412–413) is condemned to
   death as 'shameful and accurst.' In *De Doctrina* (*Col.* xv, 305)
   Christ's death is described as 'ignominious in the highest degree.'

ings upon the heavenly altar (II, 239–46) connect to and are
commented upon by Christ's presentation of the fruits of
repentance (XI, 37–8). IX, 194–6 and X, 264–73 also apper-
tain to the complex. Satan's 'hard'ning in his strength' as
he reviews the rebel host in hell (I, 572) is momentarily
shared by the reader as he is swept through the course of
Milton's greatest chivalric simile. The 'obdured breast' can
be clad in the armour of pride or more persuasively, in
the protection of 'Vain wisdom' and 'false Philosophy'
(I, 58; II, 565–9); but until the stony soil is softened, the
fruit of repentance is unable to grow. It is not only the
presentation of the repentance in Book XI (3–5) but the
basic distinction in the third book between man to whom
grace is universally accessible and the fallen angels who are
cut off from grace (183–202) which are made to bear upon
this recognition. Finally, between heaven and hell there is
limbo and limbo provides us with a contrast that has been
noted by editors.[7] The upright heart can speak directly to
its maker. The response will always reach down to the
effort of virtue, however feeble, if the upward aspiration is
authentic. But the works of 'painful Superstition and blind
Zeal' (III, 452) begin in emptiness and are addressed to the
void.

In a structure of interconnectedness, some links will be
simpler than others and the simplest by themselves may
be no more than the devout joinery of a man bringing his
sense of a pattern to the text of the Bible. But even the
simplest connections acquire dignity and ordering power
when other connections are made to surround and brace
them. The cumulative effect can only be to shape the
moment of decision more fully and to define more potently
the directions in which it radiates. Milton's careful fitting
of this scene into the whole and the multiple relevances he
is able to bring out of it are evidence of its importance, an
importance that is also apparent in the differences of the

7 Hughes, Bush, Carey and Fowler on XI, 14–16

scene from *Adam Unparadized*. These differences have
been considered elsewhere[8] and all that needs to be said
at this point is that the reshaping consistently lays before
us the full and free exercise of responsibility in the movement of the mind away from despair and back to its
forming principle. It is moreover a joint exercise; though
Adam must take the decision it is Eve who by casting her
contribution in the hierarchic mould (x, 930–1), restores the
rightness of her relationship with Adam and so enables
Adam to find his relationship with God. The identical
cadences of guilt accepted (x, 829–36) form the initial
chime of responsibility recognized and even the emphatic
spelling plays its part, taking us back across the spaces of
the poem to the emphatic *mee* of satanic egoism and the
accepting *mee* of the redemptive sacrifice.

The repentance, as we pass through it, seems to be self-
initiated. It is born of joint counsel, the discarding of
destructive possibilities, and the gradual recovery of a sense
of proportion and hope. The colouring of the experience
makes all the more crucial the parts played by will and
grace in its constitution. Prevenient grace we are told in line
three of Book xi (and significantly not until then) has made
the movement toward repentance possible. We do not
encounter this term anywhere else in Milton's poetry and
we do not even encounter it in the parallel passages which
Kelley quotes from the *De Doctrina*.[9] This may be the only
occasion on which the epic is more specific than the treatise.
One of the reasons for the specificity is to insist that the
actuality differs from Adam's understanding of it. The
grace which comes 'unprevented, unimplor'd, unsought'
(III, 231) can scarcely be the grace which Adam seeks and
for which he petitions. Adam in fact, sees grace funda-

8 *'Paradise Lost' and the Seventeenth Century Reader* (London 1947),
   78; Joseph Summers, *The Muse's Method* (London 1962), 197;
   Rajan, *The Lofty Rhyme* (London 1970), 83–4
9 Maurice Kelley, *This Great Argument* (Princeton 1961), 108, 168,
   187

mentally as forgiveness, not as a renewal within himself which he cannot initiate but without which the turn to the good is impossible.

If no more than this were happening, the movement across two books and the placing of the event in two perspectives would be abundantly and even brilliantly justified. The felt reality of the experience is one thing and the truth about its nature something else.[10] As the page turns and we look down on what has been passed through, we can define more adequately the forces that made up the movement. But there is more than this in the manoeuvre. Milton faces here a difficulty of presentation which the very success of his device makes it easy to minimise. A strong sense of the impotence of man's fallen nature, before grace makes its entry, must be combined with an even stronger, affirmative sense of man's responsibility in remaking himself. To put it slightly differently, an ethic of self-reliance must be made to join hands with a theology of dependence. The co-presence of these two recognitions with this degree of intensity is part of the shape of Milton's thought, a shape which at this point, is accessible only to a poetic translation. The solution – which is obvious only because it is before us – is to put the act of responsibility first, to give it the maximum of deliberative and dramatic weight and only then to proceed to the prior reorientation which made the exercise of responsibility possible.

In reading the repentance we are led back again and again to what it is tempting to call the dialogue at the summit. One further connection is demanded. After the primacy of mercy has been declared but before the 'rigid

10 Differing views on the relation between grace and fallen nature are offered by Dick Taylor Jr ('Grace as a Means of Poetry: Milton's Pattern for Salvation,' *Tulane Studies in English*, IV, 1954, 57, 73) and by Jackson C. Boswell ('Milton and Prevenient Grace,' *SEL*, VII, 1967, 84–94). Both views can be found instructive (though Boswell's is doctrinally more accurate) if we take one as relevant to the existential and the other to the cosmic perspective.

satisfaction' has been demanded, the relation between will and grace is stated as follows (III, 173–5):

> Man shall not quite be lost, but sav'd who will,
> Yet not of will in him, but grace in me
> Freely voutsaf't.

The 'thought' here is at least partially determined by the dramatisation, by the carefully judged interplay between the line and the sentence. The apparent finality of the first line, the stress upon 'will,' the force of effort evoked by the force of emphasis, make a psychological fact alive in the movement of language. The amending force of the second line now acts as a countermanding recognition, sweeping the understanding to the other extreme. Then the overflow turns the thought to its conclusion; the universality of the promise throws the emphasis back from dependence to responsibility, and free willing and free vouchsafing stand together in the human balance. The result is considerably more than a division of the efficient cause according to the principles of Ramist logic.[11] If we now turn to the repentance, it will be apparent that the part of the eposide given to Book x 'performs' the first line of this statement, that the part allotted to Book xi performs the second line and that the episode as a whole provides us with a far fuller sense than previously of the relationship between willing and vouchsafing. When this dramatic 'expansion' is taken together with the expansion of III, 190 over three books, we ought to respond with a heightened and energised awareness of the 'becoming alive' of pattern in existence. The process of actualization is subtle and manifold, as the many connections between Book III and the repentance suggest. To speak of it as the translation of dogma into drama is instructive but not entirely accurate. As the 'embodiments' of doctrine accumulate, they both

11 Leon Howard. ' "The Invention" of Milton's Great Argument: A Study of the Logic of "God's Ways to Men," ' *HLQ* xi (1945), 168

play against and play upon each other. The successive disclosures open out and occupy the limited area of our understanding. But as the poem puts each disclosure in its place and expounds its potencies and limitations, the final understanding takes shape as the knowledge that there is always more to be understood. The paraphrase is not the poem and while the poem through the wise use of its resources can move closer to what is seen from the highest of heights, the poem in its turn is not the vision.

It is natural that the integrity of a poem should be most firmly declared at the points most crucial to its finding of itself. Its levels of understanding and the strategies by which those levels are connected are re-enacted in the decisive moment; and as the single incident reaches upwards and outwards across the spaces of the poem we are made more creatively conscious of the force of design behind the life of detail. In a poem of the magnitude of *Paradise Lost* the manifold linkages in the web of significance are not easy to trace through and to hold in the eye of the mind. Each increment of integration widens the understanding and brings new possibilities into the field of design. Since the pattern is known only through what the pattern puts together, our sense of the poem's shape seems indefinitely renewable. This is a fact which is not without importance when we consider the poem not simply as a statement in itself but as a completed symbol of something beyond itself.

    Paradise Lost offers many routes for exploration; but the explorations suggested here are not meant to be restricted to *Paradise Lost* alone. Milton's mind has strong creative habits which can be thought of as styles of insight or distinctive ways of penetrating the subject. The relationships between the cosmic and existential, between pattern and discovery, vision and blindness, the mountain-top and the plain concern him strongly through the course of his work. These pairings are not suggested as equivalent to each other but rather as reflecting upon and extending each other. Through their interplay, the poet can put before us something of the subtlety of the union of form and experience.

In *Comus* we are made aware from the outset of the 'calm and serene air' of the attendant spirit's habitat and the 'smoak and stir of this dim world' where evil is characterised by 'eternal restless change' (5–6, 595). Within the dimness is the darkness of the wood, a 'close dungeon of innumerous bowes' (348). Darkness at midnight can lead into darkness at noon and as the emphasis moves inwards, the dungeon of man's surroundings closes around him as the dungeon of his body. *Comus* 382–4 anticipates *Samson* in this way; at the same time the contrast is made between those who cannot see at midday and those who can find their way by the steady light of virtue, even in the darkness of our condition. 'Vertue can see to do what vertue would' (372), yet the line for all its ringing confidence prescribes a limitation. The illumination provided is sufficient for error to be identified and dismissed; it is not necessarily sufficient for the pattern of creativeness to be proclaimed and understood. It is the Attendant Spirit, the representative of a different realm, who must therefore define the hierarchy of marriages which make possible the union of order and joy. The poem closes with an exhortation to ascend what Milton in his ninth sonnet calls the hill of 'heav'nly Truth' and to rise in the depths of one's being to the understanding that is possible 'above the spheary chime.'

In *Lycidas* the dark wood becomes the perilous flood and the sense of order is assaulted rather than tested. In an audacious advance of poetic strategy the differing levels of understanding are embodied in the poem's two levels of language. The progress on the ground is identified with the decorum of the pastoral order and its increasingly inade-

quate consolations. The higher mood enters the poem at its
moments of crisis, guiding the protagonist to a comprehension that is demanded by his intensity of questioning
but which is not available within the terms of his world.
These entries are managed with characteristic care. The
higher mood *descends*, touching the trembling ears of what
we can imagine as an averted face. The two-handed engine
stands at the door. If justice is from above, retribution is
from without. Both point to another realm of principles
and forces from which the rescue of the protagonist must
be effected.

The 'great vision of the guarded Mount' needs to be
considered in this context. As 'vision,' it is made to stand
apart from the pastoral world it is called on to redeem. The
assurance it offers is guarded against those sounding seas
of doubt which have raged through the poem with increasing ferocity. The amount itself is evocative of Paradise. As
the hill of truth is ascended again, the geographical sweep
of the proper names suggests the widening horizon of
understanding and the attainment of a perspective not
possible at the level of the world, or within the blindness
to which that level consigns us. As we look out on the
seas on which the Armada met its fate, the perilous flood
comes to mean deliverance as well as destruction. Death
too can pass into life and the underground river rise in
another country where the shape of things can be more
clearly discerned.

Paradise Lost begins by contrasting '*Sion* Hill' with the
'*Aonian* Mount.' The scope of his undertaking calls on the
poet to ascend to a point where he can see more clearly
and also see more of the pattern. Significantly the appeal is
for instruction, for the illumining of what is dark and the
raising of what is low. Comprehension, not eloquence is the
first gift of the muses. Comprehension is also the objective
on that hill in hell where philosophy is discussed (II,
556–61). But the debate here is a parody, not because of its

agenda, but simply because it is unavoidably a debate. Intuitive reason has fallen into discursiveness. A hill is to see from, not to contend upon.

The highest of hills transcends the notion of height and what is seen from it is seen in a simultaneous present, emancipated from the modes of space and time. From it God views his own works and their work (III, 56–9). Creation and the creation's use of its freedom are brought together and brought to rest in a pattern of ultimate and encompassing relationships the details of which are lived out as experience, or seen as fragments of understanding from the lesser hills below. Paradise stands at the crest of such a hill, safeguarded by natural and angelic defences. But Paradise itself contains more than one hill and of these the highest is the hill of history. The ascent of this hill is an ascent 'in the Visions of God' (XI, 377). It is not lower or more restricted in the view it offers than the hill on which the Second Adam is placed to be tempted by 'Earths Kingdomes and thir Glory' (381–4). The difference is less in the eminence than in the state of being of the person who stands upon the eminence. Adam is not tempted but is shown the fruit of surrender to temptation. He is offered not the power to intervene in history, but the hope that it may be redeemed from an intervention already made. The panorama below is freed from the restrictions of space and time; but the roll-call of proper names merely expounds the sonorities of tyranny. Beyond are the 'nobler sights' (411) which the power of vision makes accessible. Three drops from the well of life enable Adam to see the advance of death in the universe but also to discern the pattern of that warfare within which the promise of eternal life is offered. The grace which made possible his turn to repentance enables him to ascend that hill of vision where he can see at work in the redemption of history the same power that he experienced working in himself.

The two perspectives in which a single event in *Paradise*

Lost is seen are thus more than a locally felicitous device. The connection between them is repeatedly part of the way in which what is known is opened to understanding. In *Comus* the relationship is one of graceful contrast, with progress in the dark wood qualifying us for ascent of the hill. In *Lycidas* the two perspectives meet in the poem's collisions of decorum and language and the struggle for comprehension moves forward on the meeting-ground. In *Paradise Lost* many elevations suggest many understandings – total, partial, and parodic. What an agent knows, and what is known through what the agent knows, depends on where he stands in a sequence of actions as well as in a cosmos of meanings. In all three poems the passage through experience and the interpretation which arises from that passage are related to the vision that stands above experience; the ascent of a hill – actual or envisioned – is the final stage of the human movement to comprehension.

It would be surprising indeed if these persistent creative deployments were to find no place in Milton's final poems. How they are used and how important their uses are are matters which we shall soon investigate. Meanwhile those whose expectations have been aroused by the phrase 'final poems' are requested to live with their disappointment. This paper does not seek to intervene in the chronological dispute that continues elsewhere and that has been referred to earlier in this series. It seeks rather to build upon the indubitable fact that these two poems were published together in 1671 and that regardless of when Milton wrote them, they were the last poems which he put before his public. It may be that Milton presented these two poems in conjunction because he had nothing more constructive to do than to capitalize on the success of *Paradise Lost* by publishing something he had written and laid aside two decades earlier. But Gresham's law does not prevail in literary understanding and the sterile hypothesis should not drive out the creative one. We must at least explore the proposition that Milton put the two poems together because he meant to say something through the juxtaposition.

The title page seems at first to bear out the sterile hypothesis. It may or may not be significant that Milton describes *Paradise Regained* as a poem in four books. The Ludlow Masque, the Nativity Hymn, and *Lycidas* are assigned to a genre in their titles. But *Paradise Lost* like its successor is described only by the number of books that it occupies. More teasing is the enigmatic continuation of the title: 'To which is added *Samson Agonistes*.' Does Milton really means that his tragedy is an afterthought or that he is making up for the paucity of those four books and giving the reader due value for his splendid shilling? Or does he mean that the addition fulfills a larger integrity, that the two poems in a sense extend into each other and relate themselves to the poems that precede them, and that what is apparently thrown in for good measure is in fact indispensable to the pattern of the achievement?

The co-presence of the two poems in one volume and the contexts they provide for each other are among the facts we are called upon to celebrate. As we prepare for celebration we cannot but realize how little in the impressive outpouring of Milton scholarship bears explicitly on this problem. Samson's relationship to Christ it is true, is widely regarded as typological, though opinion differs on the events in Christ's history which are supposed to be prefigured in Milton's tragedy.[12] Unless however, the main event to be prefigured is the temptation, *Samson* while it may take its place in Christian understanding, does not

12 See in particular, F.M. Krouse, *Milton's Samson and the Christian Tradition* (Princeton 1949); T.S.K. Scott-Craig, 'Concerning Milton's Samson,' *Renaissance News*, 5 (1952), 45–53; William Madsen, *From Shadowy Types to Truth* (New Haven 1968), 181–202; Barbara Lewalski, '*Samson Agonistes* and the "Tragedy" of the Apocalypse,' *PMLA* 85 (1970), 1050–62; Lynn Veach Sadler, 'Typological Imagery in *Samson Agonistes*,' *ELH* 37 (1970), 195–210

obviously contribute to our aesthetic understanding of *Paradise Regained.* A further difficulty with a predominantly typological reading is that *Paradise Regained* nowhere mentions Samson and *Samson Agonistes* in its turn lacks any mention of Christ. The answer might be that Milton's audience was fully instructed in the typological relationship and that an artist of his tact might be expected to refrain from unaesthetic underlining of the obvious. Nevertheless confidence might be increased by the occasional reminder that the two poems were indeed concerned with this relationship. Indeed considering the typological knowledge of Milton's audience and the expectations which the two poems in one volume might provoke. it is surprising how little use he made of his opportunities. Much could have been achieved for example, as Professor Barker has reminded us, by simply reversing the order of the two poems, so that in the act of reading itself, the type was superseded by the truth. There were other possibilities that Milton chose to ignore. It seems difficult to summarily dismiss the conjecture that while the typological overtones are important, there are other relationships involved in the juxtaposition which may be at least as decisive to Milton and possibly to us.

Something can be achieved for example – and some of it has been achieved by Professor Barker and Professor Lewalski – by examining not only the relation between the truth and its type but also between the truth and its parodies. Right action – and the emphasis falls upon action – is discovered through rejection of the wrong roles.

Also persuasive is the view that Christ's trial in the desert constitutes an anatomy as well as an example, a comprehensive pattern of temptation in which all temptation can be located and understood.[13] One purpose served by juxtaposing the two poems is to establish insistently parallel structures which give this proposition aesthetic as well as

13 See Elizabeth Pope, *Paradise Regained. The Tradition and the Poem* (Baltimore 1947), 51–69

doctrinal substance. As dogma, or more stimulatingly, as the affirmation of an archetypal presence in the poetry, this view is difficult to challenge but its application calls for a firm sense of the actuality of each poem and a capacity to look for illuminating relationships rather than simple equivalences. The differing emphases in each chain of temptation and the differing strategies that are brought to bear upon the specific occasion and the suspected weakness surely mean that we must proceed with discrimination. It is one thing to recognise that a parallel can be invoked; it is another to insist obliteratingly on the aesthetic dominance of the parallel.

The proposition advanced here is not meant to displace other propositions but rather to ask what can be achieved by looking once more for the two perspectives that have been engaged elsewhere in Milton's work. It will be apparent that what we have is yet another strategic variation, testifying to the persistency of Milton's creative methods and to the underlying insights which those methods make accessible. *Paradise Regained* is concerned dominantly with one perspective while *Samson* is shaped by or made to move through the other. The relationship that is expounded as a consequence and that has already been established by the cumulative force of Milton's work is between perfection and fallibility, between the pattern possessed and the pattern stumblingly groped for, between the clarity of the completed understanding and the darkness through which the design is seen in fragments, illuminated by the lightning of the 'great event.' If *Paradise Regained* is the first poem in the sequence it is so that we can stand on the hill and know what is happening better as we enter the blindness of experience in the valley below.

Michael had promised Adam that Christ would bring 'Through the World's wilderness long wanderd man/ Safe to eternal Paradise of rest.'[14] The temptation begins

14 XII, 310–14. The lines are remembered at the close in XII, 647–8 and II, 561 is not forgotten.

significantly in the wilderness and the journey to perfection
is meant to be seen as a journey back into being. An important stage in that journey is passed when Christ declines an
epicurean banquet greatly preferable to 'that crude Apple
that diverted *Eve*' (II, 349) and to the 'cordial Julep' which
the Lady spurns in *Comus*. It is only when the order of
temptation to which Adam succumbed has been passed
through that the Second Adam is set upon his hill of history.
There he proves his fitness for action by refusing to act, or
more precisely by his readiness to stand and wait until a
higher principle calls on him to act. Commitment to that
principle is chastity in *Comus*; in subsequent and more
theological terms it is the affirmation of that divine image
which in the fall of man is overthrown but not uprooted.
The final proof of the decisive presence of that image is
when we pass beyond the presumption of knowledge that is
forbidden, to learn the potential vanity of knowledge that is
legitimate. With that last rejection the Second Adam re-
possesses for redemption the hill which the First Adam
ascended in repentance.

It is not simply in the references to Christ in the wilderness and Christ on the hill that *Paradise Lost* extends into
Paradise Regained. Many of the crucial dispositions in the
earlier poem are made so that Christ and Satan can emerge
as dramatic antagonists.[15] In the brief epic they meet face to
face to continue the struggle which determines the conditions of history. The stripped landscape and the intent combat concentrate the mind upon essentials, making us aware
that the mountain-top of clarity can also be the point where
deception is at its maximum. In these circumstances we need
to do more than glance at the ironic ignorance of I, 89–93:

> His first-begot we know, and sore have felt,
> When his fierce thunder drove us to the deep;
> Who this is we must learn, for man he seems

15 *'Paradise Lost.' A Tercentenary Tribute* (Toronto 1969), 112–14

> In all his lineaments, though in his face
> The glimpses of his Fathers glory shine

Satan's protective delusions acquire a potency compounded by his subsequent tribute (III, 9 ff.) to Christ's oracular wisdom. We have to remember the *Nativity Ode* with the special emphasis it gives to Christ's silencing of the oracles and to his rout of those pagan gods who in *Paradise Lost* are the captains of Satan's cohorts. Satan now proceeds further in his remembrance of things past that are forming the shape of the future (*PR* III, 13–20).

> Thy Counsel would be as the Oracle
> *Urim* and *Thummim*, those oraculous gems
> On *Aaron's* breast, or tongue of Seers old
> Infallible; or wert thou sought to deeds
> That might require th' array of war, thy skill
> Of conduct would be such, that all the world
> Could not sustain thy Prowess, or subsist
> In battle, though against thy few in arms.

It is not difficult to recall that when Christ ascends his chariot on the third morning of the battle in heaven he is 'in Celestial panoplie all armd/ Of radiant *Urim*, work divinely wrought.'[16] He is on that occasion called to deeds that require 'th' array of war' and the admission that 'all the world' cannot sustain Christ's prowess comes with grim accuracy from one who represents the power of the world against the power of God. The statement is also a figuring of the situation of the true church in a world of enemies; but its dramatic function is to make clear how Satan too has his blindness. The time of recognition will come – but will not come until the moment on the pinnacle.

---

16 *PL* VI, 760–1. Several critics regard these lines as specially significant since they come at the centre-point of the ten-book edition. In any case this passage and *PR* III, 14 are the only references to 'Urim' in Milton's poetry.

The pinnacle should be thought of as beyond the hill and the wilderness and as a further elevation in the ascent of being. Its false equivalent is the tower – the tower of Babel, of Satan 'hardning in his strength' and those 'proud Towrs to swift destruction doom'd' of the rebel bastions in the North of heaven.[17] Against these, the pinnacle stands as the point of ultimate disclosure where repetition is also prophecy. The suppressed violence takes us back to the battle in heaven. In the other direction, the loneliness and helplessness of the man on the eminence looks forward to the ordeal of the man on the cross. But to move backward is also to move forward and so the victory in heaven in its turn extends into the resurrection and the moment on the pinnacle.[18] Time is withdrawn into the pattern of eternity and in the complexity of the relationships which only poetry can convey, all victories open into each other and into the final victory. Satan falls smitten with amazement as he sees the true nature of his antagonist and knows what always has been and must be. It is a climax which is an act of judgement in the aesthetic as well as the ontological sense and Milton's departures from tradition not only gather together the forces of his poem but set the poem creatively in the context of his work. We see what is meant by 'deeds/ Above Heroic' and learn how Eden is 'rais'd in the wast Wilderness.'[19] 'Dream not of thir fight/ As of a Duel, or the local wounds/ Of head or heel' was Michael's caution

17 *PL* XII 38 ff.; I, 589–91; V, 907. Anthony Low, 'The Image of the Tower in *Paradise Lost,' SEL* X (1970), 17–81. Herbert is in this tradition when in *Prayer* he writes of the 'Sinner's tower' as an 'engine against the Almighty.' Jackson Cope, *The Metaphoric Structure of 'Paradise Lost'* (Baltimore 1962), 98, points out that the tower is also an 'epithet for Christ.'

18 *The Lofty Rhyme* (London 1970), 122–7; William B. Hunter Jr, 'Milton on the Exaltation of the Son: the War in Heaven in *Paradise Lost,' ELH* 36 (1969), 227; Rajan, '*Paradise Lost* and the Balance of Structures,' *UTQ* 41 (1972), 219–26

19 *PR* I, 7. The 'Waste Wilderness' reflects Hell as described in *PL* I, 60 and chaos as described in VII, 212. But we can also have a desirable wilderness, as in *PL* V, 294

to Adam on the hill (*PL* xii, 386–8). The combat of minds, the sustained obedience to a higher principle, the recognition of evil in its plausibility, the enduring of evil in its pride and dominion, and the final prevailing through a power beyond the self – these give substance to Adam's understanding that 'suffering for truth's sake/ Is fortitude to highest victory.'

If *Paradise Regained* is a poem of the hill *Samson Agonistes* is a drama of that 'subjected plain' to which the fallen Adam must descend. Its stark setting, its intricate exploration of the symbol of blindness, its rigid economy in the use of dramatic resources contribute to the feeling of confinement, of a limited world, 'prison within prison,' with only limited possibilities for knowledge. *Comus* can contrast the 'serene air' of being with the confusions of the dark wood. *Lycidas* is progressively taken over by the interventions of the higher mood. *Paradise Lost* has all time and space for its theatre and in *Paradise Regained* the prospect from the hill opens into the sweep of several empires. *Samson Agonistes* labours unremittingly in a valley which could be the valley of the shadow of death, where the angels, in a celebrated simile, are as leaves fallen from the tree of life. Samson's feeling as he begins his struggle out of his dungeon is that he too is fallen beyond hope, alienated utterly from the 'prime decree' of creativeness. There is however a preface to his situation, provided correctively by Michael before he leads Adam to that mount of speculation[20] which looks down on the fallen nature of things (xi, 349–51):

> ...doubt not but in Vallie and in plaine
> God is as here, and will be found alike
> Present, and of his presence many a signe

'Found' is perhaps the operative word. Samson cannot see God as Adam was privileged to see him in the garden and in

20 *PL* xii, 589. *PR* iv, 236 is anticipated.

the early stages of his recovery the divine presence is not
even felt. A guiding hand exists but though the spectator
can see how it guides better than the participants, the blindness of those on the stage is designed to make the audience
reflect on its own blindness. The beginning is in darkness
and abandonment. The movement back to the light can
only begin when the darkness is recognised as partially
self-inflicted and it is no accident that 'Sole author I, sole
cause' echoes not only in its form but in its cadence, the
joint repentances of Adam and Eve.[21] But to discern the
nature of the darkness is not necessarily to feel the guidance
of the light. Indeed the sense of abandonment may deepen
as the dimensions of failure are inescapably seen. The recoil
may drive one to the brink of despair before the upward
forces begin to prevail. Even then the movement back may
need to be purified of that self-castigation which finds its
centre in the wounded ego. Repentance can only discover an
anchor in a reality that lies beyond the self. The advance
into being must therefore be thought of not as a reasoned
progress, but as working through a series of situations
without fully knowing what those situations imply or what
gain has been effected in the structure of the self. 'Light
after light' is given to those who seek the way back but each
gift is for the occasion and is meant to be 'well us'd.' The
'Umpire *Conscience*' ensures that we choose rightly but
does not necessarily provide us with the reasons for that
choice.

To make these remarks is to suggest that Samson is not
Christ and not simply the shadow of Christ as earth is the
shadow of heaven. The difference between the pinnacle and
the subjected plain – subjected both to the curse of sin and
the redemptive promise – is meant to form part of the
completed understanding. The perfect man is a standard.
But the imperfect man in his blindness and vulnerability
draws us into a world of which we are natural citizens. His

21 *SA* 376; *PL* x, 832–3, 935–6

struggle involves us while Christ's victory stands above us. It is our assurance that we can draw back from destruction and that we can take part in the making of meaning, though we understand only partially the meaning that we make.

The plain nevertheless does lie in the shadow of the pinnacle in the sense that any remaking of ourselves is a maimed simulation of the recovery of paradise. We can say that Milton contributed to this relationship by juxtaposing two poems of multiple temptation (the only ones that he wrote) as well as two cases of temptation resisted. We can dutifully add, for whatever it may be worth, that in each poem the second temptation is the longest. But if we proceed on the assumption that Milton is writing a book rather than filling a filing cabinet we will need to look for more 'cunning resemblances.' Many of those resemblances are to be found in Christ's first soliloquy. A 'multitude of thoughts' swarms awakened in him; Samson's 'restless thoughts' are like 'a deadly swarm of hornets.' Christ's birth is foretold by a messenger from God; the divine portents that surround Samson's birth are repeatedly mentioned. Christ's early ambition was to 'rescue Israel from the Roman yoke' and then 'quell o're all the earth/ Brute violence and proud Tyrannick pow'r'; he prefers 'By winning words to conquer willing hearts,/ And make perswasion do the work of fear.' The Chorus in *Samson* rejoices in the discomfiture of 'Tyrannic power' and 'The brute and boist'rous force of violent men.' Finally Christ is led by 'some strong motion' into the wilderness and Samson to the destruction of Dagon's temple by 'some rouzing motions' which he feels within himself.

To ponder these affiliations is to become increasingly aware of their complexity. The swarming thoughts contrast the rich creativeness of the mind at work with the angry self-torment of the mind betrayed. We see these lacerating implications fully developed in Samson's despairing speech before Delilah's entrance. The divine portents that attend the birth of the hero contrast the covenant cast aside with the covenant about to be perfected. But the hero who violates the covenant can be restored to his office as God's champion. The valley is not the abyss and as the reader knows, perfection on the hill provides the guiding hand to lead Samson out of the shadows. Christ is offered the possibility of quelling 'Brute violence and proud tyrannic power' as Satan provides his own version of 'winning words to conquer willing hearts.' Significantly, when persuasion fails, Satan resorts to fear. The chorus in *Samson* associates 'invincible might' with 'Heroic magnitude of mind' in a phrase recalling *Paradise Regained* and with 'celestial vigour' in a phrase recalling Christ's victory in heaven. It contrasts heroic action with that 'patience' which is the exercise of saints and while moved to jubilation by the promise of the former, concludes that the latter is more probably in Samson's lot. The catastrophe combines something of both alternatives but falls considerably to one side of any attempt 'to make perswasion do the work of fear.' Lastly Christ feels the 'strong motion' within himself *before* he proceeds to his trial in the desert. Samson's 'rouzing motions' (the variation in the epithet is important) are felt *after* he has undergone his temptations. The two lines of advance can therefore not be brought into any simple relationship. They are consecutive as well as parallel, divergent as well as convergent. It is part of the proper wit of poetry to bring before us the quality of these relationships and the opening out of meaning they make possible.[22]

Complexities can fortunately co-exist with simplicity. Behind the sweep of understanding which the two poems put together we see Christ's victory standing over the subjected plain just as it does in the prospect from the hill in *Paradise Lost*. We see perfect man and man grievously imperfect, finding himself in the mire of his failings. We see

22 The passages involved are *PR* I, 196–293; *SA* 18–29, 361–4, 633–6, 1268–96, 1381–3, 1427–35

what we should be and what we can be. After Samson has struggled back to himself, lived on the edge of despair, and rejected his own past in Delilah and Harapha, we know what it means to him to trust in the living God and to find the strength that flows out of that trust not hung in his hair, but diffused through all of his being. Samson had once asked why sight was not 'diffused' in this manner. The presence of God is a deeper form of sight and the strength of his trust enables Samson to respond with confidence to the contempt Harapha pours on his situation (1168–73).[23]

> All these indignities, for such they are
> From thine, these evils I deserve and more,
> Acknowledge them from God inflicted on me
> Justly, yet despair not of his final pardon
> Whose ear is ever open; and his eye
> Gracious to re-admit the suppliant.

At crucial moments such as this, the integrity of Milton's work invites us to reach across the spaces of his accomplishment to liberate the full meaning of his words. Samson's rejoinder cannot but recall the assurance offered on the highest of heights.

> To Prayer, repentance, and obedience due
> Though but endevord with sincere intent,
> Mine ear shall not be slow, mine eye not shut.

We have seen this assurance substantiated in the turning back to goodness of Adam and Eve. We know that pattern on the hill is process in the dark wood, in the perilous flood, and in the violated garden. In the poem which stands at the end of Milton's work the assurance is again existentially worked through and the working through does justice both to the individuality of the man and the universality of the promise. The decorum of *Samson* excludes mention of grace

23 Psalm LXXXVI, 6, particularly in Milton's translation, is evoked.

in the theological sense[24] and though the restoration of the hero is compatible with and may even seem to invite a Christian reading, it must avoid announcing itself in those terms. Milton makes use of these restrictions to give us a hero whose prayer is a 'petition' for extinction and whose repentance consists primarily of recognising that he is responsible for his actions and fully deserves his punishment. 'His pardon I implore' Samson says[25] to Manoa but to seek forgiveness in this sense is not to ask for clemency. Samson lives in a world which is hemmed in by the law and loyalty to God in such a world can only mean readiness to pay the price of betrayal. The point is that the divine presence is also felt in the valley of this world, notwithstanding its limitations of prayer and repentance. The guiding hand can now lead Samson to his own rendering of 'obedience due.'

Obedience in Paradise calls only for refraining from eating one particular fruit in a garden not lacking in other means of nourishment. In a fallen world the test has to be sterner. Isolation, helplessness, and apparent abandonment to the dominance of evil characterize the climax both on the pinnacle and in the temple of Dagon; and the exposure of the man to hostile forces is accepted by the man himself. For Samson, the test also means that the 'Consecrated gift' of his returning vigour must be 'abused' in his capitulation before the herald. If he is to learn fully the lesson that his strength is not his own he must put his strength at the disposal of the power to whom he owes it. He must do so

24 *SA* 1173 is artfully within this decorum, because of the play upon the word 'gracious.' The echo of *PL* I, 112–12 is studied. Satan, excluded from grace, thinks of it and rejects it in its 'lower' signification. Samson, accepting it in the secular signification, opens his mind to the higher version of it. This would seem to be the only mention of grace in *Samson*.

25 *SA* 521. Samson is consistent in his use of 'pardon' rather than 'mercy,' notably in 1171. 'Mercy' is used only twice in the play – in an exclamation by Manoa (1509) and by Manoa at 512 in the speech to which Samson is here replying.

even if he is only dimly aware of the purposes for which that strength is to be employed. In the valley, obedience also must be blind.

The two climaxes in the final poems are carefully complementary. Christ stands on the pinnacle of the house of God. Samson tears down the edifice of the temple of Dagon. The good remains inviolable as it is in *Comus* and evil is humiliated in its noonday as it is in *Lycidas* and in the tenth book of *Paradise Lost*. We have both the sense of an ending and the sense that the ending is complete, gathering together the forces that have prevailed in Milton's work. Nevertheless, Samson's final act seems designed to remain slightly out of the reach of the reader, as if to remind him that he too is not without his blindness. This effect is achieved primarily because in Milton's play the recognition takes place off-stage, having been made to coincide with the catastrophe. The Messenger's entrance and the succession of half-truths that lead to the full disclosure, make us aware of how we can misunderstand even the physical actuality of the event. What the event means to Israel is later expounded in all its limitations. But if we ask ourselves what the 'true experience' of the event is, what it means in itself, and what it means to Samson, the answer is carefully enigmatic. We have only the Messenger's report of the moment of understanding, externally observed and even then transmitted by hearsay (1629–45).

> At length for intermission sake they led him
> Between the pillars; he his guide requested
> (For so from such as nearer stood we heard)
> As over-tir'd to let him lean a while
> With both his arms on those two massie Pillars
> That to the arched roof gave main support.
> He unsuspitious led him; which when *Samson*
> Felt in his arms, with head a while enclin'd,
> And eyes fast fixt he stood, as one who pray'd,

Or some great matter in his mind revolv'd.
At last with head erect thus cryed aloud,
'Hitherto, Lords, what your commands impos'd
I have perform'd, as reason was, obeying
Not without wonder or delight beheld.
Now of my own accord such other tryal
I mean to show you of my strength, yet greater;
As with amaze shall strike all who behold.'

The parenthesis 'For so from such as nearer stood we heard'
is meant to emphasize the Messenger's remoteness from the
event. Thus we cannot but be all the more keenly aware of
what is allowed to filter through, of the head bent in prayer,
the 'fast fixt' eyes of the blind man straining to see truly,
the mind revolving and comprehending what is to be carried
out, the 'head erect' of the man decisively aware of the
presence of the divine image in himself and the consummation of 'obedience due.' Since two links in the chain of
restoration are indicated we can even conjecture that the
third link, repentance, is comprehended in that 'great
matter' which Samson revolves in his mind. What is said on
the highest hill is once again made real in existence and the
knowledge that this is so makes 'As with amaze shall strike
all who behold' more than a piece of jubilant double-
entendre. *Paradise Regained is* in the same volume and we
are surely called on to remember Satan 'smitten with
amazement' falling from the pinnacle. Hubris and retribution attend the two climaxes and we can now see yet another
effect that becomes possible when the recognition tele-
scopes into the catastrophe. Most important, we see blindness reaching out to vision and the valley ending on the
slopes of the hill. Where we stand is less important than
how we proceed. The two poems in their contrasts and like-
nesses and in the range of embodiment that they cover are a
great poet's final declaration of the scope and depth of the
redemptive promise. All that Milton shows us after Adam

ascends the hill, the panorama of history and the prison of blindness, is meant to put around us the stern facts of our situation but also to announce, within those facts, the conditions and the unfailing presence of hope.

Milton's work has many means of creating its integrity and the two perspectives, related in various ways through the body of his achievement, are only one strategy through which that integrity is declared. To follow this strategy is instructive because it makes evident the unifying energy of the creative mind at work and the persistence over many years of that mind's basic patterns. Milton, for all the sonorities of the grand style, is not lacking in the capacity for laconic understatement. 'To which is added Samson Agonistes' must be taken as indicating that the end is both what it should be and what it was felt to be from the beginning.

THE REGAINING OF PARADISE

IRENE SAMUEL

𝕴n the usual reading *Paradise Regained* concerns what
we now call an identity-crisis; in the reading I wish to
propose it centrally concerns the choice of a life-style.[1] The
two, I hazard, are not the same, and Milton would not have
confused them. The one is exclusive, asking as the all-
important question 'Who am I?' The other is inclusive,
asking 'How is man to live?'

Since the meaning of *Paradise Regained* depends on how
we read its action, and its action depends on how we read
its crisis, our understanding of what Milton has to say
about the regaining of Paradise necessarily turns on how
we conceive of a brief passage near the end of Book IV.

1 I am indebted to the facilities of the Huntington Library, which
awarded me a grant from January through March 1971, and to the
generosity of Mr Gerald Stuart of its staff, who put at my
disposal a number of items from his own Milton collection. The
paper, designed as a lecture, remains as I read it on 30 March
1971.

Unlike *Paradise Lost*, *Paradise Regained* has been allowed
– even by twentieth-century commentators – to have an
unmistakable crisis. No one, to my knowledge, has ever
suggested shifting it from the two crucial lines where Satan,
having set Jesus on the pinnacle of the temple, taunts him
to hurl himself down, relying on the angels to rescue him,
and Jesus answers (IV, 560–1):

> Tempt not the Lord thy God, he said, and stood.
> But Satan, smitten with amazement, fell.

Commentators have further been able to agree that the
protagonist's standing is the victory foretold by the angelic
choirs in Book I and now celebrated by them in their
prophetic rejoicing over the ultimate defeat of the enemy.
But that apparently is as far as commentators will go in
agreement.

In their disagreement they have not gone appreciably
beyond two of Milton's eighteenth-century annotators.
According to one Rev. Mr Calton of Lincolnshire, 'Here is
what we may call after Aristotle the *anagnorisis*, or the
discovery. Christ declares himself to be the God and Lord
of the Tempter; and to prove it, stands upon the pinnacle.
This was evidently the poet's meaning ...'[2] Not so very
evidently, it seems, for Bishop Thomas Newton quotes
Calton only to disagree:

> I am for understanding the words, *Also it is written,*
> *Tempt not the Lord thy God,* in the same sense in which
> they were spoken in the gospels; because I would not
> make the poem to differ from the gospel account. ...
> The Tempter sets our Saviour on a pinnacle of the
> temple, and there requires of him a proof of his divinity,
> either by standing, or by casting himself down, as he
> might safely do, if he was the Son of God. ... To this our

2 Milton, *Paradise Regained*, ed. Thomas Newton (London 1752),
   IV, 561n, 182.

> Saviour answers, as he answers in the gospels, *it is*
> *written again, Thou shalt not tempt the Lord thy God,*
> tacitly inferring that his casting himself down would be
> tempting of God. *He said,* i.e. he gave this reason for not
> casting himself down, *and stood.* His *standing* properly
> makes the discovery, and is the principal proof of his
> progeny that the Tempter required.[3]

For Calton the *saying* is the protagonist's declaration of his
divinity; for Newton it is the *standing* that displays the
miraculous fact and convinces the tempter. But for both
the episode is a miracle that reveals to both agents in the
poem the divinity of the speaker-stander.

Now Calton himself had observed a discrepancy
between what he took to be Milton's handling and the
Biblical version:

> In the Gospel account ... no discovery is made of the
> incarnation; and this grand mystery is as little known
> to the Tempter at the end, as at the beginning. But now,
> according to Milton's scheme, the poem was to be
> closed with a full discovery of it: there are three cir-
> cumstances therefore, in which the poet, to serve his
> plan, hath varied from ... the Gospels.[4]

And Calton proceeds to object: (1) that according to the
Evangelists the pinnacle is not a particularly dangerous
place; (2) that there Satan only bids Christ cast himself
down, whereas Milton has him demand a proof of Christ's
special nature; and finally, that Christ's answer in the
gospels is merely the reason why he must not throw himself
down, whereas Milton has him, by directing the words
to Satan, declare himself the Lord God.

If Calton was right – and almost all twentieth-century
commentators, without sharing his objections to what

3 *Ibid.*
4 *Ibid.,* IV, 549n, 181

Milton does, agree with him[5] – Milton took the familiar episode of the temptation in the wilderness and changed its whole meaning – and this simply in order to get an adequately dramatic crisis for his poem: an *anagnorisis* or discovery for Satan of Christ's identity, with a *peripeteia* or reversal for both Satan and Christ.

Such a deliberate reinterpretation of a clear gospel text would, I wish to suggest, have been alien to Milton, wholly out of keeping with his habit. Further, I mean to hazard, Calton's reading of the scene in *Paradise Regained* is entirely unnecessary, even destructive of the point Milton intended. And Newton's answer, I will further venture, does not go nearly far enough either in meeting Calton's objections or in justifying what Milton does with the episode.

Suppose instead that Milton took the passage in the gospels exactly as other readers took it, and found it, just so, entirely to his purpose, so that he did not have to shift from the common reading or change his own habit; and suppose that the episode as Milton wrote it, without in any way contradicting the gospel narrative, makes perfect good sense. Surely it is far more likely that such a reading gives its meaning.

Newton answered Calton only on the significance Milton

5 Thus A.S.P. Woodhouse, 'Theme and Pattern in *Paradise Regained,' UTQ* 25 (1956), 181; E.M. Pope, *'Paradise Regained': The Tradition and the Poem* (Baltimore 1947), 103–4; Northrop Frye, *Five Essays on Milton's Epics* (London 1966), 149–50; Barbara K. Lewalski, *Milton's Brief Epic* (Providence 1966), 304–5, 315–19. Of twentieth-century critics, apparently only Arnold Stein, *Heroic Knowledge* (Minneapolis 1957), 130, 224–5n9, and John Steadman, *Milton's Epic Characters* (Chapel Hill 1969), 66, take Newton's view that it was the standing that proved Christ the God-man to Satan. Don Cameron Allen, *Harmonious Vision* (Balitimore 1954) takes Christ's words as a declaration of his own divinity, according to the implications of p. 118. Jon S. Lawry, *The Shadow of Heaven* (Ithaca 1968), would, I surmise, hold a view more like that suggested in this paper, according to the implications of pp. 291–302.

has Christ give to the words 'Tempt not the Lord thy God.'
From his standing fast on the 'highest pinnacle' of his
'Father's house' Jesus, according to Newton, *discovers* that
he is indeed God-man, miraculously made flesh; *ergo*, he
could not have known it when he said 'Tempt not' etc.;
ergo, he was not saying to Satan 'I am the Lord your God
and *you* are not to tempt *me*.' On this last, Newton is, I
think, entirely right: Milton would have been most unlikely
to rewrite Luke (and Matthew) and make Christ misapply
his quotation from Deuteronomy. For the phrase in
Paradise Regained is a quotation of a quotation: when the
Jesus of Luke 4.12 (or of Matthew 4.7) answers the
temptation to cast himself down, he quotes Deuteronomy
6.16 (as he quotes Deuteronomy 8.3 to answer the temptation to turn the stones into bread, and Deuteronomy 6.13
to answer the temptation to worship Satan as his God).
The commandment in Deuteronomy reads: 'Ye shall not
tempt the Lord your God, as ye tempted him in Massah.'
The reference is to Exodus 17.1–7, where the Israelites in
a crisis, doubting God's benevolence, wished to force him
to manifest himself to them by miracles. To tempt God
is thus to require miracles of him as proof of his benevolence. And the clear meaning of Jesus's quotation in Luke
(or Matthew) is that he will not ask God to intervene in
his behalf by providing a miracle. That was the common
Renaissance view of the passage, as Elizabeth Marie Pope
observes: 'Christ was tempted to make a wholly arbitrary
and unnecessary experiment of God's providence.' The
view, as Miss Pope further notes, 'squared ... with the
doctrine that he was acting [in the whole temptation-
sequence] *quasi homo*, under the same conditions as his
humblest follower.'[6] That is, the temptation sequence
in the gospels was commonly taken as exemplary, the
ground for the 'imitatio Christi' required of every man.[7]

6 See E.M. Pope, 83.
7 Cf. for example, Beza, Calvin, and Zwingli on the temptation in

Miss Pope herself does not read the episode in *Paradise Regained* thus; rather she agrees with Calton that Milton deliberately rewrote the gospel account. And of course Milton need not have conformed to common Renaissance interpretation – he departed from it often enough in his reading of the Bible. But the direction of his nonconformities was never toward greater mystery, greater miracle, but rather always toward greater rationality, greater availability as a guide in living. He was averse to making the Old Testament miraculously prophesy the New, particularly averse to unnecessary theologizing, speculation on the arcana of God, multiplication of dogma, even of doctrine, and most particularly averse to multiplication of mystery. On these matters he is unequivocal in his *Christian Doctrine (Col. xiv, 3 and 269):*

the wilderness. Theodore Beza, *Novum Testamentum*, printed at Cambridge 1642, makes clear in his marginal summary of Luke 4.1–13 how he took the temptations (p. 167):

Christus primum ad diffidentiam de Deo, deinde ad opum & bonorum studium, tertio denique ad vanam de se confidentiam à Satana solicitatus, ter cum Dei verbo vincit; priori illi Adama oppositus, solius ambitionis tentatione statim prostrato.

John Calvin, *A Harmonie upon the Three Evangelists, Matthew, Mark and Luke*, translated by E——— P——— (London 1584), harmonizing the accounts in Matthew 4.5–11, Mark 1.13, and Luke 4.5–13, is more explicit:

I had rather suspend my judgment than give the contentious occasion of quarreling. ... But this appertaineth much to the matter, to know what Sathan went about in this kind of temptation, which is to be learned by the answer of Christ. ... Christ, that he might meet with the subtlety of the enemy and beat back his force, holdeth out for a buckler, God is not to be tempted. Whereby it appeareth that the deceits of the enemy tended to this purpose, that he lifting himself up above measure, should rashly rise up against God. [p. 131] But this matter needeth no long disputation: only let us see what Christ doeth teach us by his example, which we must follow as a certain rule. ... If this clause have any force in it ... then doeth Sathan maliciously corrupt and maim the saying of the Prophet, generally and confusedly wresting the same to wandring and erroneous courses. God commandeth us to walk in our ways, & he sayth that his angels

nothing can so effectively rescue the lives and minds of
men from those two detestable curses, slavery and
superstition, [as valid Christian doctrine drawn from the
Bible]. ... [What is proposed as an article of faith] ought
not to be an inference forced and extorted from passages
relating to an entirely different subject ... nor hunted out
... from among articles and particles, nor elicited by dint
of ingenuity, like the answers of an oracle, from sentences
of dark or equivocal meaning.

He is especially vehement on any complicating of the
mystery of the incarnation (*Col.* xv, 273):

Since then this mystery is so great, we are admonished
by that very consideration not to assert any thing
respecting it, rashly or presumptuously ... not to add

shall be our keepers. Sathan pretending the custody of angels,
doeth exhort Christ that he should rashly procure him danger.
... Christ answereth most aptly, it is not otherwise to be hoped
that God doth there promise his help than if the faithful do
modestly commit themselves to him to be governed: for we cannot
otherwise trust his promises, except we obey his commandments.
... In this place he is said to be tempted, when as we neglect his
means which he putteth in our hand. For they which neglect the
means which God appointeth do as if they tried his power and
his strength. ... In sum, whosoever desireth to take a trial of the
divine power, where as it is not necessary, he tempteth God, by
bringing his promises to unjust examination. [p. 132].

Zwingli, *In Evangelicam Historiam ... Annotationes* (Zurich 1539),
takes the whole temptation in the wilderness as undergone
entirely as an example to us of modesty and temperance. On
Matthew 4 he writes: 'Post Baptismum ieiunat Christus, ut
modestiae nobis & temperantiae exemplum praeferret. ... Dat ergo
exemplum Christus, deum adesse his, quos tentari & adfligi
permittit, quemadmodum & filio suo adfuit, nam & nos filii dei
sumus per Christum' (p. p). The three temptations are (in the
order given by Matthew): *gula ac voluptas, vana gloria,* and
vana gloria and *avaritia* together (p. 9). In what he says on Luke
4 he takes the same view: 'Christus nobis tentatur, ut si quando
nos tentemur, sciamus quibus armis repellendus sit hostis.
Doctrinae suae vivum exemplar proponit. ... Omnis doctrina ...
huc tendat, ut cognitionem & amorem dei inter homines plantent,
ut homines divinam vitam vivant ...' (p. 204).

anything ... of our own; not even to adduce in its behalf
any passage of Scripture of which the purport may be
doubtful, but to be contented with the clearest texts,
however few in number. If we listen to such passages ...
how many ponderous volumes of dabblers in theology
shall we cast out ...! What is essential would easily
appear ... what is mysterious would be suffered to remain
inviolate.

And he ends his whole discussion on the mystery of the
God-man: 'it behooves us to cease from devising subtle
explanations, and to be contented with remaining wisely
ignorant' (*Col.* xv, 273). That concluding phrase stamps the
passage as essential Milton: it echoes his early letter to
Diodati (?23 Sept. 1637, *Col.* xii, 27) where he similarly
put aside another mystery with the words, 'humile
sapiamus' (Let us be lowly wise); it echoes too the grand
counsel of Raphael to Adam in *Paradise Lost* viii, 172–3:
'Heav'n is for thee too high/ To know what passes there;
be lowlie wise.'

Few critics have regarded Milton as an advocate of
'negative capability' or even of a 'wise passiveness'; yet on
such matters of ultimate mystery this was his constant
doctrine: Let us be wisely ignorant. What then would he
have said to readings of *Paradise Regained* that make its
meaning turn on sudden secret mysterious revelations
from on high to the protagonist, not one of which is
narrated in the gospels – his main source – and not one of
which is so much as indicated by a single word in his poem?
When Scripture suggests a divine revelation Milton does
not hesitate to put it in: that is how John the Baptist
recognizes the Messiah in *Paradise Regained* because that
is how the gospels say he did. So Milton writes, paraphras-
ing his source, 'him the Baptist soon/ Descried, *divinely
warned*' (i, 25–6). He does not elaborate the mystery, but

quite simply accepts it, 'wisely ignorant.'[8] But on the supposed revelation by which, according to recent commentary, his protagonist comes to know his own divinity Milton is as silent as scripture. What would he say to the subtle exegetes who have supplied an *anagnorisis*, and with it a theophany, and from that a whole action leading to the discovery of Christ's identity – all out of what he did *not* write into his poem? Something, I surmise, like what he said to the mutipliers of Biblical mysteries (cf. *Col.* XVI, 265):

> no inferences from the text are to be admitted but such as follow necessarily and plainly from the words themselves, lest we should be constrained to receive what is not written in place of what is. ...

To misquote the clear meaning of Luke – and thereby make Jesus misquote the clear meaning of Deuteronomy – would have been anathema to Milton. And would he have

8 It is the angels at the end of *Paradise Regained* who reveal to the protagonist his identity with the first-born and only-begotten Son, his past career in Heaven, the significance of his present victory over Satan for 'Adam and his chosen sons,' his coming defeat of the demonic legions; they do not speak of the crucifixion with which his earthly life will end, and they scarcely elaborate the ultimate triumph over the 'Infernal Serpent' at Doomsday. Those who have found the mystery of the vicarious atonement muted in *Paradise Regained* are right. The Son, as he reviews what he learned about himself from searching the Law and the Prophets concerning the Messiah, comments only that he found (I, 262–7)

of whom they spake
I am; this chiefly, that my way must lie
Through many a hard assay even to the death,
Ere I the promised kingdom can attain
Or work redemption for mankind, whose sins'
Full weight must be transferred upon my head.

'Even to the death' coupled with the phrase 'redemption for mankind' through the transfer of men's 'sins' full weight' suggests the full theological doctrine, but does not emphasize it or give the direction of the poem. Nor can six such lines, even when reversed his principle for the sake of his poem? But to make the sentence mean what? That Jesus is announcing his divinity to *Satan*, telling Satan not to tempt him – as though only then aware of what his interlocutor had been up to for three days – and in thus announcing and telling, declaring himself Satan's God. Who would want to be Satan's God? Not the supremely rational hero of *Paradise Regained.*[9]

If anything outside Milton's poem may be used to clarify its meaning, surely it is the companion poem, *Paradise Lost*. The key words of our brief passage, 'he said and *stood,*/ But Satan, smitten with amazement, *fell,*' with their *stood-fell* antithesis, do indeed return us to *Paradise Lost*, Book III, where the past war in Heaven is used to illustrate

supplemented by Satan's dire prediction (IV, 386–8), counter-balance the emphasis. The crucifixion simply is not a theme of major importance in Milton's poem, though it undoubtedly was in Milton's theology and in his faith. Milton is not the poet to put his main themes in glancing allusive figures. So too with the identity of the protagonist in the poem: it is a main concern of Satan, as though if he could just discover exactly who this man is he would then have the advantage of him; but God, the angels, and the man himself put their emphasis elsewhere.

9 That this is the supremely *rational* hero is clear, from the enemy's tribute to his 'virtue, grace, and wisdom' in climactic order (I, 68), through the Father's equation of his 'winning by conquest' with the opposite of Adam's losing 'By fallacy surprised' (I, 154–5), to the angels' inference that he is 'to vanquish by wisdom' (I, 173–5), and so on throughout. His wisdom, like the 'humiliation and strong sufferance' in which it will show itself, is the virtue of his reason, reason being, for Milton no less than for ancient philosophy, the capacity to discern truth and right, and wisdom being the virtue of preferring them. Consistently Platonic in his conviction that to discern the right is to prefer it, Milton often interchanges *reason* and *wisdom*, as in *PL* III, 108. At this point in Miltonic studies we need hardly even observe that when Jesus rejects Satan's 'Be famous then/ By wisdom' (IV, 221–4) he is not rejecting true wisdom or human reason but asserting them. Milton did not forget the primary meaning of *logos*, the rational spoken word, or discourse, the reason that utters itself in speech – however little he troubled about the mystical senses attached to the word by Neoplatonists and Neoplatonizing theologians.

the law of rational free will; Milton's God there asserts
(III, 102–11):

> Freely they *stood* who *stood*, and *fell* who *fell*.
> Not free, what proof could they have givn sincere
> Of true allegiance, constant Faith or Love,
> Where onely what they needs must do, appeard,
> Not what they would? what praise could they receive?
> What pleasure I from such obedience paid,
> When Will and Reason (Reason also is choice)
> Useless and vain, of freedom both despoild,
> Made passive both, had servd necessitie,
> Not mee.

The standing in *Paradise Regained* too derives from the
free choice of reason and will, as the falling derives from
the choice of unreason. To that I will return; here let me
note that Satan's falling 'smitten with amazement' also
recalls an episode in *Paradise Lost*, the end of the war in
Heaven, when Satan and his crew are driven 'thunderstruck' to hurl themselves into the abyss. The metaphor
appropriate to *Paradise Lost*, which regularly uses the large
symbol, is *thunderstruck*; in *Paradise Regained*, which
rather speaks with all possible plainness to the rational
understanding, the plain phrase is *'smitten with amazement.'*[10]

But why then did Milton choose for his poem on the
regaining of Paradise this brief episode in his hero's life? If
the episode does not end in Scripture with a theophany, nor
with a miracle that must persuade even Satan that this man
is very God, nor even with the protagonist's recognition
of himself as God made man, why make of the temptation
in the wilderness the basis for the poem? Surely Milton

10 We can even trace the shift from the metamorphical 'thunderstruck' to the literal 'amazement' within *Paradise Regained*. In
I, 35–6 Satan is 'with the voice divine/ Nigh thunderstruck'; a few
lines later, in I, 106–7, at Satan's report of this incident, his
words 'impression left/ Of much amazement to th' infernal crew.'

chose it because it was regularly taken as the ground for the *imitatio Christi* and therefore offered itself as that action in Christ's life which might be amplified and explored as defining the right way for every man. What Milton chiefly does is elaborate the temptations into arguments and the rejections into counter-arguments, so that every man may see in the exemplary answers a complete program for regaining Eden.

The exemplary answers are also detailed. In Milton's version Jesus never merely says No, much less dismisses what Satan has said as not worth answering because it is Satan who said it. He could not; for each time Milton gives Satan an argument so nearly persuasive, so close to some former thought and plan of Jesus' own at some earlier stage of his development, that only a fully reasoned answer can adequately refute the enemy's position. The Satan refuted is no mere fool, but represents the voice of the world arguing – forcefully, subtly, all but rightly – for the common, and some uncommon, views of human life. Milton intends to pit his hero against all that the world at its cleverest can say. He stresses his strength of mind, never allowing us to confuse him with the familiar sentimentalized figure of a young man pining away from a combination of anemia and hypersensitivity. Rather he makes him a 'rock of adamant,' a Herculean doer of 'deeds/ Above heroic.' We are, of course, to remember how his strength of purpose will reveal itself in his later public activity; but we are even more to observe within the poem how it reveals itself in his strength of mind. Beyond his fully reasoned answers, this profoundly rational hero can regularly diagnose the motives out of which the Satanic arguments come: 'Why dost thou then suggest to me distrust?'; 'lying is thy sustenance, thy food'; 'Ambitious spirit ... wouldst be thought my God,/ And storm'st refused, thinking to terrify/ Me to thy will.' But even finding the motive behind the Satanic arguments does not keep him from effectively answering them.

Obviously we cannot recapitulate the detail of what each says, though it is precisely the detail of what they say that makes the bulk of the poem. But if their encounter has been one long dialogue in which Satan regularly gets answered, so that he repeatedly stands 'confuted and convinced/ Of his weak arguing and fallacious drift,' from midway in Book I to late in Book IV, what in the final episode on the pinnacle of the temple so amazes him that he knows himself utterly defeated and therefore falls headlong, all his possible assaults entirely exhausted? What smites Satan with amazement in that sequence, I take it, is precisely that the man, whose special nature as 'Son of God' he has so insidiously tried to make the ground of his defeat, takes his stand *not* on his special nature at all, but on his common bond with all humanity, saying: This is the human condition, that man shall *not* ask for special miracles, as though the common ground of human life was insufficient.

In such a reading of the episode, Milton's Satan is knocked down by nothing more than an apt quotation from the Old Testament and his own surprise. It is not unlike the sequence that defeats him in *Paradise Lost* IV, when the feather-light touch of Ithuriel's spear makes him explode into his own shape, and the simple gesture of Gabriel pointing out the scale in Heaven to declare its meaning routs him from Eden, ending before it begins his desired duel at arms. Gabriel says (IV, 1006–9):

> *Satan*, I know thy strength, and thou knowst mine,
> Neither our own but giv'n; what follie then
> To boast what arms can doe, since thine no more
> Than Heav'n permits, nor mine.

As Gabriel there puts his would-be challenger to flight by his own acceptance of the very principle that is intolerable to Satan, that there is a law in the universe that holds the same for everyone, so here too the challenged man ends the combat by a simple declaration of much the same principle: let no one tempt God by asking that an exception from the

common laws of the universe be made for him. So saying,
the protagonist of Milton's poem stands – not on his own
suddenly discovered and revealed divinity, but on his completed acceptance of his common humanity.

And the joke on his adversary is that the adversary himself has made – and missed – the very point just before this
last trial (*PR* IV, 520–1, 531–40):

> All men are Sons of God; yet thee I thought
> In some respect far higher so declar'd ...
> And opportunity I here have had
> To try thee, sift thee, and confess have found thee
> Proof against all temptation ...
>   firm
> To th' utmost of meer man both wise and good,
> Not more; for Honours, Riches, Kingdoms, Glory
> Have been before contemn'd, and may agen:
> Therefore to know what more thou art than man,
> Worth naming Son of God by voice from Heav'n,
> Another method I must now begin.

With his habitual blindness he has not taken in the sense of
his own words, that all the answers given him were indeed
not only what many other men had achieved but what any
other man should be able to achieve, that the whole point
of the answers was their general truth. Everything said has
established that man as man is wholly adequate to be, say,
think, do all that man must to recover Eden, his full human
heritage. According to Satan, 'th' utmost of mere man' is
not 'worth naming Son of God'; according to Milton's
whole poem it is.

It was very much that detestable view of man that
Milton assigned to Satan back in *Paradise Lost* when he
first beheld the human pair (IV, 358–60):

> what doe mine eyes with grief behold,
> Into our room of bliss thus high advanc't
> Creatures of other mould, earth-born perhaps,

and again when he whipped himself up to the pitch of
envy-hatred required to destroy mankind (IX, 152–4,
175–8):

> Man he made, and for him built
> Magnificent this World, and Earth his seat,
> Him Lord pronounc'd ....
> this new Favorite
> Of Heav'n, this Man of Clay, Son of despite,
> Whom us the more to spite his Maker rais'd
> From dust ...

For Satan this 'earth-born' 'Man of Clay' cannot be other
than *mere* man. And 'th' utmost of mere man,' however
wise and good, cannot be *his* destined destroyer. On this
point far too many readers of *Paradise Regained*, from
Calton and Newton on down, have apparently shared
Satan's view.

Yet that is just what Milton in his opening statement
says his poem is about:

> I who e're while the happy Garden sung
> By one *mans* disobedience lost, now sing
> Recover'd Paradise to all mankind,
> By one *mans* firm obedience fully tried
> Through all temptation.

The 'deeds above heroic' prove entirely human deeds. The
first speech Milton invents for 'the Eternal Father' – to
emphasize and amplify his theme – refers to the coming
encounter between 'this *Man*' and Satan, foretelling that it
will prove him '*worthy* of his birth divine' and declaring
that what is about to be demonstrated is 'From what *consummate vertue* I have chose/ This perfect Man, by merit
called my son.' Merit, worth, consummate virtue – for
Milton's God these justify the name Son of God in the sense
that matters, the sense in which the name is earned. The
phrases echo that surprising passage in *Paradise Lost* III,
where God declares to the Son (308–11),

> [thou] hast been found
> By Merit more than Birthright Son of God,
> Found worthiest to be so by being Good,
> Far more than Great or High.

Like Satan, many readers of *Paradise Regained* take the 'great or high' – the 'birthright' – as more important than the 'merit' – and therefore as the thing to be proved. For Milton the merit is all-important, the thing worth demon-strating. That is why he has the Father speak the phrases 'worthy of his birth divine' and 'by merit called my Son' *after* the declaration at the baptism. And the angelic Choir, always in Milton quick to understand exactly the things that Satan cannot, admire and rejoice as they foretell the Son's coming triumph in 'his great duel ... / ... to vanquish by *wisdom* hellish wiles.'

To take *Paradise Regained* as centrally concerned with establishing the identity of its hero – whether for the adversary or for the hero himself – is thus to lose Milton's purpose in writing. No discovery that the protagonist is the God-man who may henceforth go about his business in full confidence of who he is could give the impulse that named this poem the regaining of Paradise and filled it with arguments and counter-arguments on possible ways of life. To read it as a 'Who am I?' poem is to limit it to a mimesis of the particular, a matter for the historian-chronicler-biographer-theologian; to read it as a 'How am I to live?' poem is to see its availability as the mimesis of a universal action, a program for every man. The mystery of the God-man is framework, accepted by the poet from the gospel story, believed, and thought of as not to be added to, complicated, or amended; the centre of the poem is the dialogue Milton invented for his two main agents.

An astute French critic of the eighteenth century, one M. R——— (probably Routh) writing *Letters Critiques ... sur le Paradis Perdu et Reconquis* (Paris 1751) objected to the poem on just this ground: 'Satan parle, Jésus-Christ répond; c'est-là tout le Poëme' (p. 258). M. R——— knew what an epic poem should be, and this was not it: an epic poem should be grand, not just morally but imaginatively, deciding the fate of nations (p. 255), whereas here 'Tout se réduit à voir la sagesse profonde de l'Homme-Dieu rendre inutiles trois ou quatre supercheries de l'Esprit de ténèbres' (p. 256). There is nothing quite like quitting the philosophers' classroom because what happens in it lacks the excitement of the bullring or the battlefield, nothing quite like despising Socrates for spending all his time talking, nothing quite like the complacency that dismisses 'profound wisdom' (la sagesse profonde) as wholly irrelevant to the 'fate of nations,' moral perhaps, but scarcely 'imaginatively grand.'

For Milton, as for a handful of other greatly imaginative writers, the threshing out through dialogue of the values in terms of which one or another way of life is to be chosen is the ultimate imaginative venture. The genre goes back, of course, to the Socratic dialogues that produced in the young Milton something like a philosophical conversion. But I have elsewhere argued the relation of Milton's poems to the dialogues of Plato; here I want to deal specifically with the value of his choosing to make of the dialogue itself the way to regain Paradise. Putting aside, then, all questions of model and influence, I take two other dialogue-sequences by greatly imaginative writers to shed light on what Milton can have meant by making Satan talk, Jesus answer, and calling that (c'est-là tout le Poëme) the regaining of man's due Eden. I take the 'Don Juan in Hell' sequence of Shaw's *Man and Superman* and the 'Grand Inquisitor' sequence of Dostoyevsky's *Brothers Karamazov*. And not because, in this, one of the figures is Christ himself returned to the world and harangued by a spokesman of the Devil's wisdom, nor because, in that, one of the interlocutors is the Devil himself harangued by an opponent who finally chooses Heaven. I take them rather because both consist in just these haranguings about just this question, What choices is a man to make so that his life may be the way to man's renewal?

Dostoyevsky's Grand Inquisitor offers a powerful argument: the only way is for the strong to take on themselves the burden, use 'miracle, mystery, authority,' and paying out bread, the means of sustenance, as a reward in their gift, prescribe for the weak in full detail the way they are to go, thus relieving them of the pain of freedom and bestowing instead the carefree pleasure of children assured by their own easy conformity that there are no hard questions and no possible demanding alternatives. The argument is not answered – or answered only by the implications of a kiss – as the returned Christ acknowledges that this new man of sorrows who wants to 'correct his work' speaks from an intolerable sense of how men destroy themselves when left free to choose their own course. The kiss is an acknowledgement, but not – even in Ivan Karamazov's own terms – an acceptance; and when Alyosha 'plagiarizes,' it comes clear that the kiss is in fact a rebuttal, an answering assertion of *caritas, caritas* being the virtue that takes others as like – not unlike – oneself. And the point, I take it, of Dostoyevsky's whole 'Grand Inquisitor' sequence is this: that all such we-they dichotomies – we the few competent, capable of the hard choices; they the innumerable incompetent, incapable of choosing for themselves – all such we-they dichotomies can be thus simply answered: we and they are so alike that no line can be drawn between us, we-they shade into each other, and the one hope is that every 'I' and 'we' will recognize the same actual weakness and potential strength, the same humanity, in every 'they' and 'other.'

Shaw's Devil too is no mean advocate of a powerful argument: since everything goes down into the abyss of nothingness, since nothing desirable remains desirable forever, let us cultivate illusion, vary our experiences, if we cannot change our pleasures multiply our partners, and by renaming everything to flatter our egos, since we cannot effectively remake the intolerable absurdity of what is, at least shield ourselves from its depressing reality. To this Shaw's assertor of the life force answers by going off to front reality and remake it; and before going he argues:

> As long as I can conceive something better than myself I cannot be easy unless I am striving to bring it into existence or clearing the way for it. That is the law of my life. That is the working within me of life's incessant aspiration to higher organization ... and clearer self-understanding. ... It is the absence of this instinct in you that makes you that strange monster called a Devil.

The Shavian Don Juan has learned from centuries in Hell that the illusions self-indulgence requires are a deadly bore, monotonous variants on one endlessly repeated theme that gets and can get nowhere; the Dostoyevskian Grand Inquisitor apparently does not learn that he is dooming all those 'children' to a kind of Shavian Hell – no problems, no responsibilities, no effort – and no possible growth. But the reader of both dialogues, I think, comes away with the sense that the great error of the two diabolical speakers is their taking men, the world, reality as immutable, and that the first step toward desirable good is to recognize the immense possible. The we-they syndrome of such self-appointed leaders as Dostoyevsky's Grand Inquisitor is like the comfort-me-with-illusion syndrome of the world's dropouts in the Shavian Hell: both take what has been as all that can be, and both take what is desirable for man as impossible.

Obviously Milton did not read Shaw and Dostoyevsky in preparation for writing his poem. What links the Grand Inquisitor sequence and the Don Juan sequence with *Paradise Regained* is first of all that all three are just talk-talk-talk. Oh, Don Juan leaves Hell at the end to go off and contemplate reality; Ivan Karamazov's returned Christ presumably leaves the Grand Inquisitor to learn that his work does not need 'correcting'; Milton's protagonist gets wafted aloft from the pinnacle, feasted and praised, his immense future predicted, before he is set down on earth to return private to his mother's house. But essentially all that has happened is just talk, the objection made against *Paradise Regained* by that M. R———, and innumerable others – though not, surprisingly, against the other two dialogues.

It is partly to obvert this objection, I surmise, that commentators have mostly treated the talk in *Paradise Regained* as less important than the amount of space Milton gives to it. Eager to find an action that justifies the poem, they have treated the talk as though the mere formula of rejecting temptations were enough to get from the beginning, the proclaiming of the 'beloved Son' from Heaven, to the ending, the angelic choiring of the 'True Image of the Father.' But then, why so much elaboration of the arguments and counter-arguments? Why so much waste of words in invented discussion – and so little narrative of the familiar biography? Surely a poet's intention is to be known by what he chooses to elaborate and deliberately invents, not by his glancing allusions to what everyone already knows and comes prepared to supply. What Milton invents in *Paradise Regained* is almost entirely what this one said and the other replied – just talk – and not merely to flesh out the poem, but to give it its being.

The explanation is, I think, something like what Hannah Arendt has said in a quite different connection (*On Revolution*, New York 1963, 222):

> What saves the affairs of mortal men from their inherent futility is nothing but this incessant talk about them, which in its turn remains futile unless certain concepts, certain guideposts for future remembrance, and even for sheer reference, arise out of it.

Milton would not have recalled the affairs of men inherently futile, as Hannah Arendt does; but he too thought talk about men's affairs the necessary preparation to dealing with them, and the better the talk the better the preparation, since from such talk concepts can emerge to serve as guideposts, and not only for remembrance and reference, but for choice and possible deed. If *Paradise Regained* consists so largely of such incessant talk it must be that what is said in detail seemed to the poet, who gave these things to his agents to say, of immense importance, importance immense enough to warrant his naming his poem the regaining of Paradise.

For to Milton's mind, saying is itself a doing, and demonstrating a conviction by fully reasoned argument of itself means that the conviction will be enacted. *Paradise Regained* assumes that no one does act against his real convictions; and it assumes too that convictions are willing to support themselves with reasoned argument. Even Satan makes his habitual resort to force only after his arguments fail. Even he would like to win the battle of the mind. He cannot because his opponent spots the error in his two sets of arguments, one set resting on the supposed unalterability of things, the other on the special nature of the appointed leader of men.

In *Paradise Regained* the second set of arguments fails because the man proclaimed as special near the beginning of the poem and celebrated as unique at its end, repeatedly insists throughout the dialogue on his likeness to other men: 'Is it not written/ Man lives not by Bread only?' The same power that kept others alive in the wilderness he too can rely on. Again, 'Men endu'd with ... [Virtue, Valor, Wisdom] have oft attain'd/ In lowest poverty to highest deeds' – as witness Gideon, Jephtha, David, Quintius, Fabricius and others. 'And what in me seems wanting, but that I/ May also in this poverty as soon/ Accomplish what they did, perhaps and more?' Or again, 'true glory [is]

when God/ ... with approbation marks/ The just man' – for
example, Job and Socrates; and this is all the glory a wise
man wants. Or again 'What wise and valiant man would
seek to free/ These thus degenerate, by themselves en-
slav'd?' And again, 'many books/ Wise men have said are
wearisom; who reads/ Incessantly and to his reading brings
not/ A spirit and judgment equal or superior/ ... Uncertain
and unsettl'd still remains/ Deep verst in books and shallow
in himself.' (This last has caused endless trouble, though if
we take it straightforwardly as meaning that a man needs
no particular body of knowledge in order to know how he
ought to live, the statement is self-evident.) The adversary
is constantly saying, Since you are the exceptional man ...;
and the protagonist as constantly answering, What holds
for all men *holds* – and therefore for me as well.[11]

The other ground that the adversary persistently argues
from is the unalterability of things: You'll have to eat
first; but you've got to eat, don't you? Or, There's no way
of doing anything in this world without money. Or, Only
a name-person can get to the point of achieving anything;
better get yourself known. Or, You'll need power, and the
way to power is military conquest. You'll need authority,
and for that you must have high office. You'll have to
persuade everyone to everything, and to do that you'll have
to know precisely the 100 best books they know. And
repeatedly the ground of the answer is: the world is no
such limited uniform unalterability as you assume; the
past has in fact contained evidence of manifold possibilities
that suggest manifold other possibilities that men have
hardly begun to try; man is not caged in a world he never
made, but makes his world – badly if he assumes such
compelling necessities in the nature of things – and can
remake it – better if he reexamines those supposed necessities. It cannot all be done at once; nothing done at once
is done for ever; and nothing worth putting into the human

11 We can hardly forget that according to the gospels Jesus taught
his followers to say 'Our Father.'

heritage can be imposed. Only the human life fully lived
can accomplish the things worth accomplishing – since the
life fully lived communicates the convictions on which it
lives until others live by such convictions too and com-
municate them until they become the tissue of life among
men. An imposed order changes nothing essential; the
essential changes come from growth (in Milton's Christ's
phrase, 'like a tree' spreading o'er all the earth), an organic
growth that simply by being replaces 'All monarchies
besides throughout the world.'

These are, of course, counsels of perfection that the
protagonist of *Paradise Regained* speaks; and that no
doubt is another main reason why even careful Miltonists
prefer to read the poem as biographic-particular rather
than ethical-universal: it is so much easier to take the
arguments as appropriate exclusively to the one extraordinary speaker than to accept their applicability to every
man. But Milton has placed that view too, that hard truths
hold only for the exceptional person; he assigns it to
Satan (I, 478–83):

> Hard are the ways of truth, and rough to walk,
> Smooth on the tongue discours't, pleasing to th' ear
> And tuneable as Silvan Pipe or Song;
> What wonder then if I delight to hear
> Her dictates from thy mouth? most men admire
> Vertue who follow not her lore....

The words are preliminary to the hardest truths of the later
dialogue, as though Satan were protecting himself in
advance with this assertion that the hard ways of truth
are prettinesses to please the ear, admirable nonsense that
no one could be such a fool as to ask others to take
seriously. Oddly enough, that is the way many readers of
Paradise Regained take the hard truths that follow, though
the one way of admiring virtue, the poem declares, is
precisely to 'follow her lore.'

The usual reading of *Paradise Regained* makes it an

easy-exclusive poem; what I am suggesting is that it is both inclusive and hard. The usual reading rests on assumptions like those of Dostoyevsky's Grand Inquisitor: freedom of choice is only for the exceptional; the rest need miracle, mystery, and authority. Milton, I submit, saw such dichotomies of the human race as Satanic, assuming a we-they that makes the restored Eden impossible. Like Shaw's protagonist, Milton's is willing to go on talking, even to the Devil, confident that out of right talk can come a vision of 'something better,' which man will then 'strive to bring into existence.' Reasoned argument is his means, the 'I' of his argument everyman, and the assertion of every man's adequacy his purpose.

Such a reading of *Paradise Regained* makes it, of course, essentially Socratic. According to William Blake's familiar epigram, 'If morality was Christianity, then Socrates was the Savior.'[12] Blake, we remember, had to create a myth in order not to be enslaved by other men's. Milton, on the contrary, thought the heritage of the world's wisdom needed only 'th' up-right heart' and the reasoning intelligence to end every sort of enslavement. For him, Christianity is at least morality. He therefore creates a highly Socratic Saviour to enact through dialogue the adequacy of 'mere man' to the regaining of the fully human Paradise.

12 From *Laocoon, Poetry and Prose of William Blake*, ed. David V. Erdman (Garden City, NY 1965), 272.

AGON AND LOGOS

Revolution and Revelation

NORTHROP FRYE

Milton intended *Paradise Lost* to be a Christian conquest of the Classical epic genre, and similarly *Samson Agonistes* is a Christian conquest of the Classical genre of dramatic tragedy. In Classical literature, as in Classical life and culture generally, there are, as Milton sees it, two elements. One is a development of natural human ability, or what we now call creative imagination, outside the Christian revelation, and therefore possessing, not the truth of that revelation, but an analogy of or parallel to that truth. Although the poetry of the Bible, according to *The Reason of Church Government*, is better as poetry than Classical poetry, the latter is a safer model for poets not sure of receiving the highest kind of inspiration. But Classical culture is not simply a human development, unfortunately: man without revelation cannot avoid accepting some demonic version, which means parody, of that revelation. Hence such forms as the Homeric epic and the Sophoclean tragedy are genuine models of style, decorum, and 'ancient liberty'; at the same time they are also connected with something ultimately demonic, a pseudo-revelation from fallen angels. The use of Classical genres by a Christian poet should show in what respects they are humanly analogous to the forms of Christian revelation, and in what respects they are demonic parodies of them.

In *Paradise Regained*, a brief epic for which Milton mentions no Classical model, the sense of parody is at its sharpest. Christ can overcome the temptations of Satan because he can clearly see the demonic taproot of everything Satan offers. I have never understood why Christ's rejection of Classical culture in that poem was such a puzzle to critics: it seems so obvious that in that context Christ has to reject every syllable of it. It does not mean that *Milton* is rejecting it: it is only because Christ does reject it that Milton can accept so much of it. The rejection of the English dramatic tradition in the Preface to *Samson Agonistes* is much harder to understand. The theme of *Paradise Regained* is, appropriately, a parody of a dragon-killing romance, or, more accurately, it presents the reality of which the dragon-killing romance is a parody. For Milton, of course, there is no strength except spiritual strength, and no conflict except mental conflict, hence the prophecy that the Messiah will defeat the serpent can only be fulfilled by a dramatic dialogue.

In *Paradise Lost*, too, so far as we can think of it as an epic modelled on Homer and Virgil, the sense of parody is much sharper than the sense of analogy. The Classical epic is a poem of heroic action, of *klea andron*, brave deeds of men. Christianity has a completely opposed notion of what a hero is: a Christian hero is one who imitates or approximates the heroism of Christ, which consisted in suffering, endurance, and compassion. The sense of opposition doubtless greatly intensified in Milton's mind between his discussion of Christian heroism in *The Reason*

of Church Government and the writing of *Paradise Lost.*
In the latter poem, in any case, the conventional heroics of
the Classical epic are mainly transferred to Satan and the
other devils. There is, it is true, a great war in heaven in
which the faithful angels perform prodigies of valour, but
when on the third day the Son of God disposes of the
entire rebel host single-handed, the sense of parody is
strongly reinforced. The whole war in heaven is really a
joke to God, for whom any strength apart from his will
does not exist. The same sense of the identity of strength
and divine will, along with the unreality of any strength
apart from it, recurs in *Comus,* where the elder brother
explains how the Lady's chastity is an invincible strength,
and in the Samson story itself, where Samson kills a
thousand Philistines 'With what trivial weapon came to
hand,' the jawbone of an ass (142–3).

Paradise Lost*, as I have said elsewhere, restates in
Christian terms, reversing the pagan ones, not only what
a hero is but what an act is. For Milton the only genuine act
is the act performed according to the will of God. Adam's
eating of the tree of knowledge was therefore not an act,
but the pseudo-act of disobedience; the revolt of Satan was
the parody-act of rebellion. The only genuine actions in
Paradise Lost are those performed by the Son of God,
the acts of creation and redemption. The same principle,
applied to *Samson Agonistes,* will help to explain Milton's
conception of tragic action. Nothing really happens anywhere except the accomplishing of the will of God. In the
world of the angels above man this will can be clearly seen
as a benign providence: in the world of animals below man
it can be seen in a kind of reflecting mirror, as the automatic accuracy of instinct. As the working of God's will
is relatively uncomplicated in these worlds, there is no
possibility of anything like tragic action, as Milton
conceives it, among either angels (faithful angels, of
course) or animals.

In human life too it is still true that nothing really happens except the accomplishing of God's will, or what we call providence. But there – or here – the will of God is much harder to see, because it is concealed by the powerful current of pseudo-acts released by human passion and demonic instigation. God's providence can be seen by the human reason, but the reason, being normally a submerged and suppressed critic of a dictatorial passion, is seldom attended to. The three levels of reality are indicated by the Messenger when he says (1545–7):

> But providence or instinct of nature seems,
> Or reason, though disturb'd and scarse consulted,
> To have guided me aright, I know not how.

They also appear in one of the choral odes, where God is told that in relation to man he (670–3)

> Temperst thy providence through his short course,
> Not evenly, as thou rul'st
> The Angelic orders, and inferiour creatures mute,
> Irrational and brute.

Human life sets up a kind of perpetual Saturnalia or inversion of the providential order in which the wicked flourish and the good are persecuted or ridiculed. For the most part we have to wait for a judgment after the end of life, whether of an individual life or of human history itself, in order to see good vindicated and evil confounded. But every once in a while the wicked do meet with appalling disasters in a form which makes it clear to the eye of reason that the disaster is the consequence of previous folly or arrogance. The good, merely because they are good, are in for a rough time in human society: their normal fate is, at best, ridicule or neglect, at worst martyrdom. The good man, or prophet as he usually is, is an agent of a counter-counter-movement in human life, of God's will working against human evil, and his life may well be tragic in relation to that evil, which often claims him as its victim. Yet the good may occasionally be recognized as having been right even through the torrent of lies and illusions which is the normal course of history.

We have tragedy when it is possible for the human reason, in contemplating the fall of Belshazzar or the justification of Job, to catch a glimpse of the working of God's will in human life against the power of human passion or evil. Tragedy is thus, for Milton, the recognition of God's will by human reason in the form of justice or law. As justice or law is an equalizing or balancing principle, its emblem being the scales, the tragic vision has the equalizing effect that Aristotle calls catharsis. The consequences of human passion cannot be seen as tragic by human passion, but only by human reason, which casts passion out of itself by seeing a greater passion before it, on the principle of like curing like in homeopathic medicine. That is, in the soul passion normally dominates reason; in tragedy passion is externalized, in a position where only reason can recognize it; the effect of catharsis is thus to revolutionize the soul, restoring reason to its ascendancy and casting out passion by passion.

There are, as is obvious, at least two levels of tragic action. The lower level, in which disaster appears to be the inevitable consequence of folly or wrongdoing, is what is expressed by the word nemesis in Greek tragedy. This kind of nemesis-tragedy has already happened to Samson before *Samson Agonistes* begins: it belongs to a play that Milton gave a title to but did not write, Samson Hybristes. In the play that we have this nemesis action is the tragic action so far as it affects the Philistines. Samson himself goes through a redemption in which he is accepted once again as an agent of God's will and a champion of Israel. Hence, though he is inevitably involved in a tragic death, it is not a death to which the conception of nemesis is any longer relevant.

The tragedies of the Philistines and of Samson are, respectively, the elements of demonic parody and of analogy in the tragic action. What happens to the Philistines is the same kind of thing that happens to such figures as Ajax in Sophocles or Heracles in Euripides, where the causes of catastrophe are, ultimately, devils. Samson, on the other hand, is a human analogy of Christ, of whose death his death is a prototype. It follows that the central area of tragic action, for Milton, is the Old Testament, where the Christian reader or audience may see the higher kind of tragedy in its true perspective, as part of the analogy of the law.

This conception of two levels of tragic action however recurs in Greek tragedy, most explicitly at the end of the Oresteia. Here there is a nemesis movement represented by the Furies, who are not capable of distinguishing the elements of equity in a tragic situation, such as the amount and kind of provocation given by the victim, but are the unleashing of an essentially automatic force, the righting of a disturbed balance in nature. This nemesis movement is overruled by a legal decision in which gods and men are included, and which is the higher tragic vision of the whole action, ending in the acquittal of Orestes. Similarly in the two Oedipus plays: Oedipus tears out his eyes in a kind of reflex revulsion of horror, without stopping to consider that his own unconsciousness of the guilt he has been involved in is a point of some ethical relevance. The action of *Oedipus Tyrannos* goes through a self-discovery which moves backwards in time and ends in blindness; *Samson Agonistes* goes in the opposite direction, through a progressive and forward-moving self-discovery away from blindness. It therefore runs parallel (to a very limited degree) with the action of the second Oedipus play.

We first see Samson in the throes of nemesis, tormented by the mechanical furies of his own conscience. Christian ethics has always distinguished remorse from repentance (*metanoia*), and although there is genuine repentance in Samson, the sterile brooding, the self-chewing which is what 'remorse' literally means, is more prominent at first. Just as Samson's body is infested by vermin, so all the mental vermin engendered by the lord of flies (the devil Beelzebub, invoked by Harapha) are infesting his mind, producing there what at times suggests an allegorical reading on Milton's part of the torments of Prometheus (623–4):

> Thoughts, my Tormentors, arm'd with deadly stings
> Mangle my apprehensive tenderest parts.

Samson has been tempted and has lost, and the result of losing a temptation is demonic possession. The Chorus is puzzled by the fact that Samson is so much worse off than they are: there seems to be a kind of manic-depressive rhythm in nemesis which ensures that the bigger they are, the harder they fall. This is of course the wheel-of-fortune rhythm in tragedy that so fascinated medieval writers (681–91):

> Nor only dost degrade them, or remit
> To life obscur'd, which were a fair dismission,
> But throw'st them lower then thou didst exalt them
> high –
> Unseemly falls in human eie,
> Too grievous for the trespass or omission.

The overtones of this last line would take us a long way – into the Book of Job, for example. But to the main point the answer, or part of the answer, is that those elected by God are capable of sin in a way that ordinary people, or what the Chorus calls the 'common rout' (674), are not. This is *a fortiori* true of Adam in Eden, for whom the most trivial of trespasses, by ordinary human standards, was also the greatest possible sin. Yet even he could not fall as low as the devils, who fell from a greater height. The same principle applies in reverse to the Philistines. The divine vengeance on them extends primarily to their lords and priests: in the destruction of their temple 'The vulgar only scap'd, which stood without' (1559). The wheel-of-fortune rhythm for them may be heard in the two off-stage noises, the shout of triumph and the death-groan, which we hear as the wheel turns a half-circle.

The nemesis of Samson takes the form of 'captivity and loss of eyes,' and the action of the play, we said, so far as it affects Samson, moves away from nemesis. Manoa has elaborate plans to free Samson from captivity, and he also expresses the hope that God will restore Samson's eyesight along with his strength. Much of this is only the facile hopefulness of a rather weak man, but it is true that symbolically Samson's freedom and vision are both restored. They are restored within the realities of his situation, which means that the process is full of tragic ironies, starting with the reversal of Manoa's picture of how the restoration might take place. But it does take place none the less. At the beginning of the play Samson is a slave in both external and internal bondage: besides being 'at the mill with slaves,' he is in a 'Prison within Prison,' and is, as the Chorus says, 'the Dungeon of thy self' (41, 153–6). None the less he asserts his spiritual freedom, negatively, by refusing to take part in a Philistine festival, and then positively by accepting the dispensation that God gives him to go, of which more later. At the temple itself he performs various feats in obedience to commands, but the crucial act he performs 'of my own accord,' as a free man. Similarly, although in his blindness he possesses an internal light, such as Milton claims for himself in the *Second Defence* and elsewhere, he is well aware that, as the Chorus says, it 'puts forth no visual beam.' But in his final enterprise he is, according to the Semichorus, 'with inward eyes illuminated' (163, 1689).

In the Book of Judges Samson's final prayer is 'let me

die with the Philistines.' Milton does not quote this directly, though it is the theme of Samson's speech to Manoa, but he does ascribe to Samson a most eloquent longing for death. This longing in itself is despair, but God transmutes it to a heroic achievement ending in death. God is thus acting in accordance with the same homeopathic principle, of casting out salt humours by salt and the like, which is part of the catharsis of tragedy. And in proportion as Samson is released from nemesis, the whole nemesis machinery is transferred to the Philistines. It is they who acquire the hybris or 'spirit of frenzy' which is the normal condition of the Greek tragic hero, and with the last line of the first Semichorus, 'And with blindness internal struck' (1686), the transfer is completed.

The 'spirit of frenzy' is associated with drunkenness, the 'jocund and sublime' Philistines being a contrast in this respect to the water-drinking Samson. It is still morning, but, as Milton remarks in the Commonplace Book, people who are habitually drunk can get drunk without the aid of wine. This drunkenness however is a Dionysian drunkenness, an enthusiasm or possession by a god, or what they consider a god. The Bible says of Samson that his hair began to grow again when he was in the Philistine prison-house. There are few concessions to probability in folk tales, yet we may perhaps ask the question: once the Philistines had learned the secret of Samson's strength, why did they allow his hair to grow again? Two answers are suggested by Milton. One, the mill owners were making a good deal of money by exploiting his labour, 'The work of many hands,' as Samson calls it. Two, the Philistines really believed in the power of Dagon, and therefore believed that Samson's strength could be contained within limits convenient to them. It was this belief in particular that was their 'spirit of frenzy.'

The King James Bible says that Samson was commanded to make sport for the Philistines, and, as the schoolboy

added, he brought down the house. The New English Bible
makes it clear that what Samson had to do was fight, like
a gladiator. The two translations are not inconsistent:
elsewhere in the Old Testament (as Huizinga points out
in *Homo Ludens*) to 'play' or 'make sport' can mean to fight
to the death. But gladiatorial fighting would not have
suited Milton's conception. Dramatically, Samson would
not want to spoil his climax by killing individual Philistines, but, more important, Milton says more than once
that when Samson had his genuine strength, no single
person dared oppose him. Hence the behaviour of Harapha.
The model for Harapha's character is his son Goliath, and
while Goliath is certainly a boaster – it was conventional
for warriors of his type to begin with boasts – there is no
indication that he is a coward. He expects King Saul to
come out to meet him, the Saul who was said to be head
and shoulders over every man in Israel, and when David
turns up with his slingshot he is genuinely disappointed as
well as contemptuous. During the colloquy with Harapha
Samson suddenly asserts his role once again as a champion
of Jehovah, and Harapha does not dare pursue the matter
further. He may, of course, have been a coward all along,
but it may be that something more than simple cowardice
is breaking him down.

It is essential to Milton's dramatic purpose, then, that
Samson in the temple is purely an entertainer, almost the
buffoon, of a Philistine carnival, an *agonistes* in the sense
of a performer or actor – hardly as a contestant in games,
for he is not competing with anyone. At the same time
he is a tragic hero, a defeated champion, and an *agonistes*
in that sense, to his Danite followers. The action moves
quickly through what Yeats would call a double gyre, as
the tragedy becomes a triumph and the carnival a shambles.
It is this aspect of Samson's situation in particular that
makes him a dramatic prototype of Christ, for Christ is
also a tragic hero to his followers as well as a mocked

and ridiculed figure of a carnival to his enemies, and the same reversal of action occurs there.

In *Samson Agonistes* the reversal is expressed in a complex imagery of light and darkness. Milton knew too much Hebrew not to pick up the overtones of *shemesh*, the Hebrew word for sun, in Samson's name, and perhaps he saw something of a solar-shaped myth in the story of the long-haired hero who fell into the dark prison of the west. The play opens at sunrise with Samson physically in the open air, but, like other titans, including Prometheus at the end of Aeschylus's play, he seems to be symbolically in a kind of subterranean prison or 'interlunar cave,' and the very rare classical allusions in the play link him with Atlas and Ixion. It is almost as though Samson, or a power guiding Samson, were moving under the world like the sun at night, back to the place of its rising. The action ends abruptly at noon, with the zenith of the Philistine triumph suddenly blown to pieces by the explosion of a dark hidden fire rising like the phoenix from its ashes. From the Israelite point of view, this means that the 'total eclipse' Samson complains of has lifted and that although 'he seems to hide his face,' the true sun-god has unexpectedly returned.

Samson Agonistes is a real play, with a real plot and real characters, and it could be acted with success, I should think, in front of any audience ready to accept its conventions. Yet Milton said that it was not intended for the stage, a statement often connected with the prejudice against stage plays among extreme Puritans in England. The prejudice itself is not very interesting nor particularly relevant to Milton, but the traditions behind it are more so.

What Milton would call paganism is a religious development focussed on visual symbols. Polytheism is impossible without pictures or statues to distinguish one god from another. As a pagan society becomes more centralized, it converges on a capital city, such as Gaza is described as being, and the visual worship of gods is supplemented by various forms of spectacle, including a strong concentration on the supreme ruler or king as a visible symbol. Hebrew religion is founded on revelation, which means revelation through the ear. In the theophanies of the Old Testament, God speaks and man listens, but the status of what is visible is much more doubtful. Even where the vision is expressly said to be of God, which of course for Milton would mean the Son of God, the description is always of something or someone else, variously described as an angel, a spirit, or simply a man. Much of the vagueness in Milton's conception of the Holy Spirit is simply the result of his accepting literally the ambiguities in such passages. God is, in himself, invisible, and hence, as the first two commandments enjoin, no permanent image of him should ever be made. Thus in the story of the burning bush, the visual object, the burning bush itself, is there only to catch Moses' attention: what is significant is what is said. We are told that God spoke, but that the angel of the Lord appeared; that Moses had no trouble listening to God, but could not look at him.

The shift of metaphors from eye to ear, in other words, introduces into religion the conception of idolatry, and this in turn is the source of two characteristics which separate the Biblical tradition from the pagan one. These are the dialectical and the revolutionary. Polytheism, even when it takes the form, as it did with the Philistines, of concentrating on a single national deity, has the kind of tolerance that is the result of intellectual vagueness, because the conception 'false god' is very difficult for it to assimilate. At the same time it is also conservative and authoritarian, because its religion is ultimately the authority of the state. The Philistines have both lords and priests, but it is clear that the lords have supreme power. The Bible was produced by a subject nation never lucky at the game of empire, and it looks forward to a future in which the great powers of the earth, along with their gods, will be overthrown. The visual metaphors are transferred to this future state: the 'day of Jehovah' in Judaism, the second coming in Christianity, are occasions that will be openly visible to the faithful. Hence the objections of early Christians, including Tertullian and Lactantius, to the games and contests of the Roman circus, which, apart from their brutality, focussed attention on the power of the secular state and its heathen cults. It was essentially the visual stimulation in them that was dangerous, and the title of Tertullian's attack has a visual emphasis: *De Spectaculis.* Tertullian urges his readers to avoid all such entertainments and concentrate on the better spectacles afforded by Christianity, the future second coming of Christ and the Last Judgment. Milton refers to this passage in his Commonplace Book in a way which makes it quite clear that he has no use for the blinkered bigotry that lumped in the plays of Sophocles with gladiatorial fights as equally 'stage shows.' But of course the fundamental Christian emphases are also his.

The visual image is centripetal: it holds the body immobile in a pose of static obedience, and sets the sign of authority before it. The revelation by the Word is centrifugal: it is primarily a command, the starting-point of a course of action. In the Biblical view everything we can see is a creature of God, and a secondary repetition of the primary Word of God: *fiat lux, et fuit lux.* Adam was surrounded with a visible paradise, but what the forbidden tree primarily forbids is idolatry, the taking of the visible object to be the source of creative power, as Eve does when after her fall she bows in homage to the tree. Since the fall, paradise has been an invisible inner state, to be brought into being by the revelation through the Word. The Word not only causes all images of gods to shrivel into nothingness, but continues to operate in society as an iconoclastic force, in other words a revolutionary force, demolishing everything to which man is tempted to offer false homage. To revert to the burning bush story, God there tells Moses that he is entering history, giving himself a Hebrew name and a specific and highly partisan political role, the role of delivering an oppressed class from the constituted authority of their oppressors. Further, God defines himself existentially as 'I am,' not essentially as He Who is, so that there is no possibility of Hebrew religion ever depersonalizing its supreme God, as Classical religion tended to do in Stoicism and elsewhere.

As Christianity became a social institution, the Tertullian prejudice against visual stimulation relaxed somewhat, and in medieval Christianity there is again a strong emphasis on the visual symbols which are the normal sign of a secure and confident society. This emphasis on the visibility of the Church was followed in its turn, in some areas of Protestantism, by an iconoclastic reaction which con-demned the use of images, the decoration of stained glass and sculpture, and the visual focus of the elevated host, and therefore, of course, revived the old condemnation of spectacles in theatres. Milton was no William Prynne, but he was a revolutionary iconoclast whose instinct, in attacking the government of Charles I, was to centre his attack on the visual image of royalty, and on the dangers of that image as a potential source of idolatry. Hence he could hardly avoid reflecting some of the same anti-visual tendencies that were present in his cultural milieu. In fact, if he had been able to read T.S. Eliot's unfavourable contrasts between his aural Baroque rhetoric and the 'clear visual images' of Dante, he might even have said that the clear visual images of Dante indicated how badly Dante's version of Christianity, to say nothing of Eliot's, was in need of reformation.

In this world the essential conflict between good and evil takes the aural form of a conflict between the Word and the oracle, true and false rhetoric. Yet the ultimate object of all false rhetoric is a visual image commanding obedience

to something other than God. Thus in *Paradise Regained*
Jesus enters a desert, with no visual features to distract
him, to engage in a mortal combat with the false word, the
accuser. But Satan can only operate by summoning up a
series of visual hallucinations. If Christ were to accept
any one of these, he would instantly have become identified
with it, according to the Psalmist's axiom about idols:
'They that make them are like unto them,' which is echoed
in *Paradise Lost* in the passage about the metamorphoses of
the devils (x, 540–1):

> what they saw,
> They felt themselves now changing.

Samson Agonistes exhibits a parallel conflict between
the Word of God within Samson, the ultimate source of his
strength, and the temptations of the accuser, which take the
form of a sequence of dialogues. The importance of this
aspect of the conflict is one of the things that Samson's
blindness symbolizes. Samson lives in a kind of seance-
world of disembodied voices, between the mill with its
slaves and the temple with its lords: as he says of the
Chorus (176–7):

> I hear the sound of words; thir sense the air
> Dissolves unjointed e're it reach my ear.

Everyone who speaks to Samson, including Manoa and the
Chorus, has something to add in the way of reproach, something to suggest distrust or uncertainty, something of
Eliot's 'loud lament of the disconsolate chimera' heard by
the Word in the desert. Even Samson's hearing has to be
mortified: he can only break from Dalila by, so to speak,
putting out his ears. Greek tragedies of course also concentrate on dialogue and have catastrophes reported by mes-
sengers, but still a Greek play, with its masks and amphi-
theatre setting, is a very intense visual experience, as the
etymology of the word theatre reminds us. The action of

Milton's play, like that of the Book of Job, forms a kind of visual anti-play. In this respect it anticipates some of the techniques of a later dramatist who has also often been called a Puritan, Bernard Shaw. Superficially it seems like a discussion of past and future events without any action at all except what is offstage. More closely examined, the action is there all right, but it is a curious kind of internalized action: the important events are going on invisibly in Samson's mind.

Meanwhile, the Philistines are preparing their festival of Dagon. I have been calling the building that Samson destroys a temple, because that is symbolically what it is, a place for the celebration of the Dagon cult. But of course it is also a theatre, as the Messenger calls it, a very un-Athenian theatre where the entertainment is like that of a Roman circus. The Philistine programme committee, like so many of its kind, has not engaged its chief attraction until the last moment, which explains, if it does not excuse, the frantic mixture of bluster and promises in the Officer's message. So Samson is removed from an action of which his mind is the circumference to a theatre in which, blind and unable to stare back, he is the visual focus for the whole Philistine society, the gaze of Gaza, so to speak. But by that time he is once again an agent of God, and it is very dangerous for a Philistine society to make a visual focus out of that. We remember that Tertullian urged his readers to withdraw from actual spectacles and feast their minds on the tremendous firework show promised in the Book of Revelation, when all their enemies would be seen burning in the lake of fire. In the famous passage about literary genres in *The Reason of Church Government* (*Yale* 1, 812 ff.), the Scriptural model for tragedy is said to be the Book of Revelation ('intermingling her solemn Scenes and Acts with a sevenfold *Chorus*'). Nothing could be less like the Book of Revelation than *Samson Agonistes*, and yet, with its seven great choral odes (it has seven characters also, counting the Chorus as one), its subject is a prototype of the underside, so to speak, of the vision of that book, the aspect of it that comes to a climax in the elegy over the fall of Babylon in chapter eighteen. The identification there of the city of Babylon with the Great Whore who says 'I am a queen, and no widow,' and the emphasis on merchandise and shipping, perhaps indicates a larger significance for the role of Dalila and the elaborate ship imagery attached to her. This larger significance is anticipated in *Paradise Lost*, with its comparison of the fallen Adam and Eve to Samson and 'Philistean Dalila.'

The visual emphasis that Milton distrusts as potential idolatry exists in time as well as space. In time it takes the form of an anxiety of continuity, which produces the doctrine of apostolic succession in the Church and the principle of hereditary succession in the state. The belief that all matrimonial contracts have to be treated as unbreakable is a by-product of the same anxiety. Apostolic succession replaces the spiritual succession of those called by God with the mechanical continuity of a human office; hereditary succession similarly destroys the divine principle of the leadership of the elect. The genuine king, like the genuine prophet, emerges when God calls him. The succession of leaders and prophets is discontinuous in human terms, and no human devices will safeguard it. Thus, according to the opening of the Gospel of Matthew, Jesus was legitimately descended from Abraham and David through his father Joseph, and yet Jesus was not the son of Joseph. Samson was one of a line of heroes called by God when his people turned again to him after a period of apostasy. The calling is represented by a very beautiful annunciation story in the Book of Judges, which ends with the angel returning to heaven in the fire on an altar. This image, twice referred to in *Samson Agonistes*, modulates into the image of the phoenix, the image of divine succession, a unique power of renewal through total self-sacrifice which cannot be programmed, so to speak, by any human institution.

One play that I often think of in connexion with *Samson*

Agonistes is Racine's *Athalie*, another great seventeenth-century tragedy on an Old Testament subject. The connexion is largely one of contrast, *Athalie* being a spectacular play with crowds of characters: like Byron later, in a very different way, Racine thinks of the Old Testament not as the desert of the law but as a source of Oriental glamour. We notice too how *Athalie* turns on the issue of hereditary succession through the youthful prince Joash, who is in the Davidic line leading to Christ. In this, if nothing else, Racine resembles Shakespeare, whose histories in particular so strongly emphasize the crucial importance of a clear line of succession. I suspect that the prominence of this theme in Shakespeare is one reason why Shakespeare has so little influence on the tragic drama of Milton.

The Biblical narrator remarks of the age of anarchy following Samson: 'In those days there was no king in Israel; every man did that which was right in his own eyes.' The Old Testament never quite makes up its mind whether hereditary kingship was a good thing for Israel or not, but still the glories of the reigns of David and Solomon are made much of, and it is easy for a Christian reader to see in these royal figures the prototypes of Christ as the world's only really legitimate monarch. Certainly the distinction between the person and the office, which Milton makes so much of in the regicide pamphlets, is derived from the Old Testament's attitude to kings. In *The Reason of Church Government* there is a long allegorical passage describing the king as an unfallen Samson, an image about his long hair being echoed in *Samson Agonistes*. The inference seems clear that Samson, so long as he was a leader chosen by God, was not merely a legitimate king but may at one time have had the power to set up the kingdom of God on earth, there being no limits to the divine strength which was the source of his. One of the remarks about Samson made by the Chorus brings out this larger dimension of his significance (173–5):

But thee whose strength, while vertue was her mate,
Might have subdu'd the Earth.
Universally crown'd with highest praises.

If *Samson Agonistes* did not exist, we could say with
some confidence that Milton could never have chosen
Samson for a hero, because Samson is the only important
Old Testament figure who simply will not fit into Milton's
conception of the Old Testament. The statement remains
essentially true even after we see how Milton has trans-
muted his hero. The stories about Samson in the Book of
Judges are savage and primitive even for that very savage
and primitive context. The Chorus does the best it can with
Samson's chief and not very amiable virtue of total ab-
stinence from wine, but it can only celebrate his feat of
tearing up the gates of Gaza by suppressing the reason for
his spending the night there. In nearly all the folk tales related to the Samson and Dalila motif, the part of Samson is
played by an ogre or cannibal giant whom everyone is glad
to be rid of, and the vicious and lethal practical jokes that
Samson plays on the Philistines clearly roused a reserved
admiration in Milton, even though he shared the bias of the
Biblical narrative. Milton tells us that Samson, as he
gropes for the pillars of the temple (1637–8)

stood, as one who pray'd,
Or some great matter in his mind revolv'd.

We know from the Book of Judges that the subject of his
meditations is a plea for private revenge, 'only this once.'
This also has to be suppressed, as no catastrophe involving
the will of God, for Milton, can take place without manifesting the axiom 'Vengeance is mine,' which belongs to a
higher morality than the Biblical Samson can reach.

For Milton the Old Testament is the book of the law, and
it is extraordinary to see how the wild berserker of the
Book of Judges has been so tamed by Milton that he can

find his way through a surprising amount of casuistry. The nicest legal points of the limits of civil obedience to a spiritually hostile power, of the obligations of a wife to a husband of a different nation and religion, of the relation of a deliberate action necessarily involving death to wilful suicide, of the distinction between command and constraint, are raised and debated with great skill in the play, most of them by Samson himself. Another set of associations of the Greek word *agon* is with law cases, where *agonistes* means advocate. This aspect of Samson connects with the legal metaphor in the Bible by which the conception of a redeemer developed out of words meaning an ally in a lawsuit or trial.

Samson has to work his way from bondage to liberty through the law, and hence to some extent he recapitulates Milton's own programme for the people of England. Questions of religious, domestic, and civil liberty are the main issues raised in his colloquies with Manoa, Dalila, and the Philistine Officer. From the beginning Samson is marked out in contrast to his followers who prefer 'Bondage with ease to strenuous liberty.' In worldly terms it is the maddest paradox that Samson, being worked to death as a slave in a Philistine mill, is actually closer to freedom than he would be living at ease in retirement at home, but as God conceives of liberty this is none the less true. Thus Manoa's proposal, made out of the most genuine love for Samson, is still a very subtle and dangerous temptation, as is more obvious when it is repeated, in a more sinister context, by Dalila. Dalila, of course, represents the threat to domestic liberty in its crucial form of marriage to an idolater. The Bible does not call Dalila Samson's wife, but in Milton she must be a wife to absorb his divorce arguments. The Officer's summons brings the whole dialectic of liberty in an ungodly world into a dramatic focus. So far as the Philistines are Samson's secular overlords, they have a right to his obedience; so far as he is being ordered to join in an act of worship to Dagon, they have none. Samson

decides that what he is being summoned to is a religious
event, and refuses to take part in it.

In *Paradise Regained*, after Christ has refused all of
Satan's temptations, Satan sets him on the pinnacle of the
temple, where he remains miraculously poised. Miraculously, because he has done all he can; what he has done
has been accepted by the Father, and the Father moves in to
sustain him at the crucial point. On a smaller scale, the
Lady in *Comus*, still paralyzed after repudiating Comus, is
miraculously saved by Sabrina, according to the promise
of the last two lines of the masque:

> Or, if Vertue feeble were,
> Heav'n it self would stoop to her.

Samson has also done what he can and has also come to the
end of his own will. As noted previously, during the encounter with Harapha Samson reasserts himself as a champion of Jehovah, and Harapha slinks off, perhaps because
he was a coward anyway, but more likely because Samson's
claim has been accepted. Samson is, like Jesus in *Paradise
Regained*, a man under the law, and to an exceptional
degree because of his Nazirite vow. The nearest that any
Old Testament character can get to the freedom of the
gospel is a dispensation, when God transcends his own law,
and moves his elect to do the same. Samson's first marriage
to the woman of Timnah was such a dispensation. We are
not told, either by Milton or the Bible, that his marriage to
Dalila was one too, but if it were, the dispensation to Samson parallels the dispensation to Hosea, made for very
different purposes, who was ordered first to marry a 'wife
of whoredoms' and then to 'go again' and love an adul-
teress. The fact that God has fully accepted Samson once
again is marked by another dispensation, when God's will
takes over Samson's will and changes his mind about going
to the festival. Of course, this moment also makes it certain
that Samson will die, just as the moment of Christ's
triumph over Satan makes the Crucifixion certain. Hence it

is not only the crisis of the action, but the peripeteia or turning point of the tragedy. Samson says (1372–9).

> If I obey them,
> I do it freely; venturing to displease
> God for the fear of Man, and Man prefer,
> Set God behind; which, in his jealousie
> Shall never, unrepented, find forgiveness.
> Yet that he may dispense with me, or thee,
> Present in temples at idolatrous rites
> For some important cause, thou need'st not doubt.

The word 'yet' may well be the most precisely marked peripeteia in the whole range of drama.

A second major change that Milton makes in Samson's character is in his relation to society. In heroic literature there is often a narrative tension, and sometimes a moral tension as well, between the themes of war and of quest. There is, let us say, a central war going on which it is the duty of heroes to engage in, but the crucial hero, whose presence is necessary for success, has withdrawn from the action or is on some private venture of his own. The role of Achilles in the *Iliad* comes readily to mind: much closer to the general tone of the Samson stories in the Bible is the situation in Ariosto. Here the heroes who are supposed to be fighting in a crusade, defending Paris against the infidels, keep wandering off and rescuing attractive heroines in remote quarters of the earth, and the climactic action, reminding the modern reader of the American crusade against Communism, is a trip to the moon to recollect some scattered heroic wits. In *Paradise Regained* the crusade and the lonely quest are united in the person of Christ, because for Milton Christ is the only figure in history in whom they could have been united.

Samson in the Bible is a pure quest figure: he lounges about the Philistine countryside killing and destroying and burning crops and sleeping with their women, but with no hint of any organization behind him. He might even be

called a manifestation of Philistine unrest. The final sentence in the Book of Judges, 'He judged Israel twenty years,'
comes as a considerable shock: *that* Samson has never
shown the slightest capacity to judge anything, much less
lead a nation. But in Milton all Samson's exploits are carefully integrated into a consistent crusade for God's people
against God's enemies. To the Chorus' reproach, 'Yet *Israel*
still serves with all his Sons,' Samson responds, 'That fault
I take not on me' (240–1), and goes on to show that the
failure of his people to follow him was as crucial as his own
failure. The same awareness of his social surroundings
comes out even in details. When the timid Chorus expresses
uneasiness after Harapha's departure, and again after the
first exit of the Officer, Samson quiets their fears very un-
obtrusively, but in a way which shows the born leader
under all the rags and filth and chains.

Samson's role as leader makes clear many things about
Samson Agonistes, beginning with its date, which some
people have tried to put earlier than 1660. The death of
Samson, though tragic, points to a world above tragedy; the
destruction of the Gaza aristocracy, though tragic, or at
least 'sad,' as Manoa says, points to a world below it. In
between is the tragic failure of Israel to live up to its role as
God's people. In many tragedies there is a non-tragic point
of escape indicated in the action, a moment of opportunity, of taking the tide of fortune at the flood, and the
missing of this point is part of the parabola shape of
tragedy, the point from which the catastrophe, which
means the downward turn, begins. Near the end of the play
Manoa says that Samson (1714–16)

> to *Israel*
> Honour hath left and freedom, let but them
> Find courage to lay hold on this occasion.

But the Bible tells us that in a few years the Philistines were
stronger than ever. In the Book of Judges, the account of
Samson is immediately followed by another story about the

Danites in which, after appearing in a most contemptible light as idolaters, thieves, and murderers, they vanish from history. In Jacob's prophecy of the twelve tribes at the end of Genesis, Dan is described as treacherous, and in the list of the twelve tribes in the Book of Revelation the name of Dan is omitted. For Milton this would practically mean being erased from the book of life.

The tragedy of Israel, and of Dan in particular, is an allegory of the tragedy of the English people, choosing a 'captain back for Egypt,' and deliberately renouncing their great destiny. The self-identification of the blind Milton with the blind Samson is impossible to miss: it is there in the complaints about poverty and disease, its furthest reach being perhaps the curious parenthesis about fair-weather friends: 'Of the most I would be understood.' But there may be some also with the hopeful and bitterly disappointed Manoa, if we think of the great image in *Areopagitica*: 'Methinks I see in my mind a noble and puissant nation rousing herself like a strong man after sleep, and shaking her invincible locks' (*Yale* ii, 557–8). This is precisely Manoa's picture of Samson miraculously restored to his strength as though the Dalila episode had been only a bad dream. In *Samson Agonistes* we are sombrely reminded not only of the original story of Samson, but of the fact that it was so brief and so ineffectual an episode in the history of Israel. Within a generation after the death of Dan's great champion, Dan had effectively ceased to exist as a tribe. No once favoured group of people, whether Danites in Israel or Puritans in England, is likely to get a second chance to renounce its destiny.

In the criticism of Shakespeare we notice how much of what is written really amounts to a rationalizing of the acting. What is said about characters, repetition of imagery, or the mood and emotional tone of the play, is very often potentially a set of suggestions for some producer or group of actors to consider for a possible performance. The on-

tological status of such criticism is a matter of some interest,
especially to those who believe that there is such a subject
as hermeneutics. For *Samson Agonistes* the critical situation is considerably altered by the presence of a chorus. A
chorus in the play is primarily a stylizing of the audience.
The Chorus in *Samson Agonistes*, like Job's friends, represented a kind of moral norm. They are on the right side, and
are carried along by the action to genuine profundity and
eloquence at the end, but, like so many of Jesus's disciples,
they never fully understand the meaning of the events they
are involved in. They function as eyes for Samson, but they
do not see what he sees. Some of the verse given them to
speak seems to me to be doggerel, or, if that is too violent a
word, an indication that the highest kind of spiritual insight
is not being expressed.

From the point of view of the Chorus, the action of the
play is a melodrama with Jehovah as hero and Dagon as
villain. Jehovah is the true God: somehow or other the
Philistines ought to know this; somehow or other they
ought to accept, as a valid argument, Samson's explanation
of his attack on them (1211–13):

> I was no private, but a person raised
> With strength sufficient, and command from Heav'n,
> To free my Countrey.

Samson's act is cited by Milton in his *First Defence* as a
precedent for the Parliamentary revolution. When God
himself is a partisan actor in history, it is not difficult to
hear in the background the tedious self-righteous cry:
whatever we do is right because we're we, and they, after
all, are only they.

Against this is the creative imagination of the poet
working out his play, and giving to every aspect of that
play its own realization. It is particularly in the last speech
of Dalila that we can understand how Milton is a true poet,
and of Dalila's party without knowing it, at least as long

as he is speaking with her voice. The Chorus says smugly, 'A manifest Serpent by her sting' (997), but we are bound to have some dramatic sympathy, if not moral sympathy, with Dalila in her desperate attempt to restore her self-respect, after Samson's bitter and contemptuous rejection of her, by building up a fantasy about her future fame. However we see her, we can understand that she sees herself as a kind of Antigone, damned whether she does or doesn't. When she designs a memorial for herself in language anticipating Manoa's design for Samson's tomb, we concur in the imaginative symmetry, just as we do in *Paradise Lost* when Moloch persuades Solomon to build him a temple opposite Zion. When she compares herself to Jael, we can agree that Jael's act was also treacherous, if less cold-blooded than hers. Above all, when she appeals to Fame to justify her, we can see, at least for the moment, that although Fame seems the most arbitrary and whimsical of all gods, still there is a rough justice in his (or her) dispositions, and that he averages out to a more fair-minded god than the jealous Jehovah.

Then we come back with a shock to realize how much of Milton himself is standing in the *choros geronton*, agreeing with them that God's ways are just and justifiable. For most modern readers, I should think, Milton's creative imagination is always right and his justifying apparatus always wrong: the imagination is that of a poet who is for all time; the apparatus comes from seventeenth-century anxieties which, at least on their political side, were as dead as mutton even before *Samson Agonistes* was written, to say nothing of three centuries later. Yet the imagination would probably never have conceived a line without the driving force of the anxieties. What is our final role as readers? Do we simply try to deliver the immortal poet from the 'prison within prison' of the anxieties of his age and class, or can we find a place for them too in our response?

The answer begins with the fact that we have our own

anxieties too, and that they are unlikely to meet the test of time any better than his. The task of criticism is neither to leave such a work as *Samson Agonistes* sitting in the seventeenth century, ignoring all the reasons for its appeal to us, nor to annex it to our own age, ignoring its original assumptions. The two points of 1671 and 1971 form the base of a triangle of which *Samson Agonistes* itself is the apex, in a world above both, though related to both.

Milton describes the action of *Paradise Lost*, at the beginning, as 'this great argument,' and the action of *Samson Agonistes*, at the end, as 'this great event.' The question whether Christianity and tragedy are compatible has often been raised: the real question however is not that, but the relation of tragedy to a revolutionary attitude. I have tried to indicate very briefly the revolutionary qualities of the Biblical tradition which were followed so closely by Milton: its conception of God as having a historical role in delivering a subject nation from its overlords; its iconoclasm; its insistence on right belief, and its utter repudiation of all gods except its own. *Paradise Regained* and *Samson Agonistes* are both, in different ways, set within the human situation, and they therefore express the central revolutionary attitude, in both religious and social contexts, that Milton held and expressed in his prose writings.

The revolutionary mind does not reject tragedy, but it prefers to think of it as explicable, as something with a cause, and therefore, if possible, a cure. It is apt to get impatient with the contemplating of a tragic situation as an ultimate mystery at the heart of things. *Paradise Lost* is among other things an attempt to account for the origin of tragedy: it deals, rather more coherently than Nietzsche was later to do, with the birth of tragedy from the spirit of music. In the third book, however, Milton shifts the scene to the angelic order, above tragedy, where God explains the human situation from that perspective. Here Milton deserts the revolutionary point of view of his own religion, which means that, not being an angel, he is compelled to adopt the rival perspective of the pagan world. The model for the God of Book Three is Zeus in the *Odyssey*: nowhere in the Bible does God speak in such a tone. Still, the effort to gain a larger perspective on tragedy in *Paradise Lost* is deeply significant.

The supreme Greek god, from Homer to the Stoics, is, we said, an essential God, He Who is; the God of the burning bush is an existential I am. We may perhaps suggest, however simplistic it may sound, that when God is conceived as essential, tragedy becomes existential, and vice versa. In Greek literature tragedy is inherent in the human situation, and it is that partly because in the long run the gods can shrug it off or detach themselves from it. For Milton, no tragic action can take place without the will of God being directly involved, and therefore tragedy, for Milton, is ultimately explicable in terms of God's revelation. Writers who elude this antithesis, notably Shakespeare, cannot have a decisive influence on Milton's tragic form: Shakespeare's tragedies are not religious in so specific a sense.

So when the Chorus describes itself at the end of the play as being equipped (1755–6)

> with new acquist
> Of true experience from this great event

it is possible that, once again, the Chorus does not fully understand what it is saying. It is seeing the death of Samson much as a Greek audience might see the end of *Oedipus at Colonus*, as a deep and awful mystery, something to be contemplated as a vision. It sees the hand of God in it, of course, but in a way that deepens the sense of mystery. The Danites see only as far as the old dispensation allows them to see. For Milton, and ideally for us, the words 'new' and 'true' carry a heavier weight of meaning: true experience is something that leads to renewed action, as the experience of losing Lycidas led his friend 'Tomorrow to fresh woods, and pastures new.' As the blinded Samson says to the sighted Harapha, in a line with a dozen kinds of irony in it: 'The way to know were not to see but taste' (1091). Like the Chorus, we are led to 'calm of mind, all passion spent,' but we are not necessarily old and tired and blinkered by the law. When catharsis dissipates, for an instant, the clouds of passions and prejudice and anxiety and special pleading, some of us may also catch a glimpse of a boundless energy which, however destructive to social establishments, is always there, always confronting us, and always the same, and yet has always the power to create all things anew.

This book

was designed by

ELLEN HUTCHISON

under the direction of

ALLAN FLEMING

University of

Toronto

Press